Iran in the Changing World:
Outsiders' Perspective

Iran in the Changing World:
Outsiders' Perspective

Printed in	2019. 09. 16.
Published in	2019. 09. 20.

Author	Cargi Erdem, Jung Soo Seo, Yoonmin Kim
Edited by	Jung Soo Seo
Publisher	Synn Ilhi
Published by	Keimyung Unversity Press – www.kmupress.com Rm 112, Industry-Academic Cooperation Hall Keimyung University, Seongseo Campus 1095 Dalgubeoldaero, Dalseo Gu, Daegu 42601 TEL. +82-53-580-6233 FAX. +82-53-580-6235
Registration	1970. 9. 1.(#347-1998-1)

ISBN 979-11-89468-89-7 93300
Price: ₩16,000

Iran in the Changing World:
Outsiders' Perspective

Edited by **Jung Soo Seo**

KEIMYUNG UNIVERSITY PRESS

CONTENTS —

Acknowledgement · 6

List of Abbreviation · 8

The Contributors · 10

I Iranian Foreign Policy towards the Korean Peninsula in a Time of Change: Challenging Perspectives · 14
Cagri Erdem, Keimyung University

II The Korea-Iran Relations in Trade and Foreign Direct Investment: A Review of the Past for the Future · 54
Jung Soo Seo, Keimyung University

III Islamic Banking in Iran · 96
Yoonmin Kim, Keimyung University

ACKNOWLEDGEMENTS —

This book is a collection of the three research efforts: two papers presented at the 2017 Arts and Humanities Conference on the Silk Road and Central Asia, Keimyung University, organized by Academia Via Serica (then the Centre for Silkroad and Central Asia) and one invited paper. This book fundamentally presents about outsiders' perspective on Iran in this changing world.

Cagri Erdem wrote about the origins of Iranian foreign policy since the 1979 Revolution, emphasizing Iran's cultural identity. He argued that Iran's recent 'Looking East' strategy, particularly toward China, and also in that context Iran's complex relationship with North and South Koreas, reflect Iran's efforts to escape international isolations, thus appealing to Iranian policy makers as a viable alternative.

Jung Soo Seo presented Korea's trade and foreign direct investment (FDI) relationship with Iran, a major oil producer and a faithful crude oil supplier to Korea, a natural crude oil deficient country. Seo argued that the bilateral trade relationship between Korea and Iran has been complementary, and that Iran has been as an outlier for Korea's FDI when Korean firms and businesses have formed its production networks in the Asian region.

Yunmin Kim focused on the aspect of the Islamic banking and finance in Iran and highlighted that the banking system in Iran has been an effective tool of pursuing Islamic economic objectives. But, he argued, it has been plagued with inefficiency, and thus Iran needs to introduce new financial products and instruments for the banking system in line with innovations in modern banking in order for the Islamic banking to continue contributing to the welfare of people and the community in Iran.

LIST OF ABBREVIATIONS —

BRIC	Brazil, Russia, India, China
DPRK	Democratic People's Republic of Korea
OFDI	Outward Foreign Direct Investment
G20	Group of Twenty; Argentina, Australia, Brazil, Canada, China, France Germany, India, Indonesia, Italy, Japan, Republic of Korea, Mexico, Russia, Saudi Arabia, South Africa, Turkey, the United Kingdom, the United States, the European Union
G7	Group of Seven; Canada, France, Germany, Italy, Japan, the United Kingdom, the United States
GCC	Gulf Cooperation Council; Bahrain, Kuwait, Oman, Qatar, Saudi Arabia, the United Arab Emirates
GDP	Gross Domestic Product
GFC	Global Financial Crisis
HCI	Heavy and Chemical Industry
IAEA	International Atomic Energy Agency
ICBM	Intercontinental Ballistic Missile
IMF	International Monetary Fund
IR-SLBM	Intermediate Range Submarine Launched Ballistic Missile
LNG	Liquefied National Gas

MENA	Middle East and North Africa
MINT	Mexico, Indonesia, Nigeria, Turkey
MRBM	Medium Range Ballistic Missile
PPP	Purchasing Power Parity
USSR	Union of Socialist Soviet Russia
WMD	Weapons of Mass Destruction

THE CONTRIBUTORS —

Cagri Erdemis an assistant professor at Keimyung Adams College of Keimyung University, Korea and received DEUG, Licence and Maitrise degrees in Administration Economique et Sociale (AES) from Université de Montpellier-III, France, obtained his BA and MA in International Relations at San Francisco State University and Ph.D. in political science from Syracuse University of New York. Previously, Erdem worked at British Aerospace Engineering (BAE) Systems and at Dogus University, Istanbul as an assistant professor.

Jung Soo Seo is an associate professor in the School of Economics and International Commerce, Keimyung University, Korea. He received his MA and Ph.D in economics from School of Economics, the University of New South Wales. He previously worked at the Australian Defence Force Academy and at the University of New South Wales.

Yoonmin Kim earned his Ph.D. at Claremont Graduate University.

Currently, he is an assistant professor in the School of Economics and International Commerce, Keimyung University, Korea, publishing his works in International Money and Finance, International Political Economy and Behavioral Finance, etc.

Iran in the Changing World: Outsiders' Perspective

I

Iranian Foreign Policy towards the Korean Peninsula in a Time of Change: Challenging Perspectives

CargiErdem, Keimyung University

I

Iranian Foreign Policy towards the Korean Peninsula in a Time of Change: Challenging Perspectives

Cagri Erdem

Abstract —

There is no doubt that the international system is going through a period of rapid transformation. Thus, the global distribution of power—political, economic, military, and cultural—is also changing. An increasingly complex world where the global and the local meet presents us with new challenges and opportunities. This study investigates the changes taken place in Iranian foreign policy since the Revolution of 1979 and explores how the Islamic Republic of Iran is coping with new challenges/opportunities presented by those dramatic global transformations. In that regard, 'Looking East' did prove to be a viable alternative for Iranian foreign policymakers. Moreover, despite the unusual alliances and conflicting political ideologies, Iran has been among the few countries in the world that have sustained close and continuous relations simultaneously with both South and North Koreas, forming an unanticipated web of complex relations on the Korean Peninsula for some decades now. Consequently, it accentuates the complexity of prophesying international politics and offers unusual perspectives on Iranian foreign policy vis-à-vis the Korean Peninsula.

Keywords
Iran, Korea, Middle East, foreign policy, Korean Peninsula, East Asia, nuclear power, international security, energy, missile technology

Introduction —

Throughout the last several decades, some important events have caused fundamental changes in the political world. The 1990s witnessed a number of high profile incidents revealing all the warning signs of uneasy transition, such as the sudden end of the Cold War, the disintegration of the Union of Soviet Socialist Republics (USSR or a.k.a. the Soviet Union) and the ethnic cleansings in Rwanda and former Yugoslavia. The same trend continued in the early decades of the 21st century through the September 11, the Iraq war, the 2008 global financial crisis, the Syrian/Iraqi civil war, the Arab Spring, and the rise of China. Following the transitional period after the collapse of the USSR, the world witnessed the rise of new regional powers challenging the hegemonic status of the United States in particular and the western world in general. This led to the coining of the terms such as BRIC[01]—Brazil, Russia, India, China—or MINT[02]—Mexico, Indonesia, Nigeria, Turkey. We can no longer rely on a firm guidance of G-7[03] countries alone regarding global economic affairs. Currently, G-20[04] countries play a more significant role for coordinating the direction of the global economy. Although that sort of categorization(s) confined mostly to increasing economic capabilities, its concerns also strayed into the realm of political and military affairs. The present

---

01 BRIC is an acronym coined in 2001 by the former chairman of Goldman Sachs Asset Management, Jim O'Neill for Brazil, Russia, India, and China.

02 This term MINT (Mexico, Indonesia, Nigeria, and Turkey) was initially coined by Fidelity Investments, a Boston-based asset management firm, to draw attention to their economic growth potentials in the 21st century.

03 The Group of Seven (G7) is an informal bloc of almost entirely western industrialized democracies--the United States, Canada, France, Germany, Italy, Japan, and the United Kingdom--meeting on a regular basis to discuss issues such as global economic governance, international security, and energy policy. However, currently, in the absence of the Russia and China, it is mostly an outdated structure without any real relevance.

04 The G20 membership is composed of the world's largest advanced and emerging economies, representing about two-thirds of the world's population, 85 per cent of global gross domestic product and over 75 per cent of global trade.The current respective members of the G20 are Argentina, Australia, Brazil, Canada, China, France, Germany, India, Indonesia, Italy, Japan, Republic of Korea, Mexico, Russia, Saudi Arabia, South Africa, Turkey, the United Kingdom, the United States and the European Union.

political turmoils in the Middle East,[05] South China Sea,[06] Korean Peninsula,[07] Eastern Europe,[08] and Central Asia[09] are all manifestations of a more assertive role played by those newly rising regional powers challenging the status quo established after World War II. Those rising powers from the developing world emerge as the main actors in regional politics, and they face a highly institutionalized world order established and maintained by and for the United States and its allies.

Scholars who study how 'rising powers' affect the international system

---

05 There are numerous ongoing conflicts in the larger Middle East: Libyan Civil War (2014-Present) between various factions challenging the new government; Yemen War and Foreign Intervention (2014-Present) as a result of a rebellion against the government by the Houthi Shiite tribes in the north and the response of the coalition of Sunni Arab states including Saudi Arabia, the United Arab Emirates, Egypt, Jordan, Bahrain, and others (who are in a cold war/proxy war on several fronts with Shiite Iran) by a sustained bombing campaign against the Houthis; Islamic State War (2012-Present) Islamic Jihadist group that evolved out of al-Qaida in Iraq controlling significant portions of Iraq and Syria.

06 The South China Sea disputes involve both island and maritime allegations among several sovereign states within the region. China, Vietnam, the Philippines, Taiwan, Malaysia, and Brunei all have competing claims.

07 The Korean peninsula is the pivot in Northeast Asia's balance of power equation. From a geopolitical point of view, it is located in the heart of Chinese, Japanese, American, and Russian vital national interests. Consequently, it would be fair to categorize the peninsula as an arena prone for great-power confrontation.

08 There are some worrisome circumstances causing instability in Eastern Europe such as the annexation of the Ukrainian territory of Crimea by the Russian Federation on 18 March 2014, the sporadic clashes in parts of Donetsk and Luhansk provinces in the Eastern Ukraine between pro-Russian and Ukrainian government troops, the Russian threats to the Baltic States, and NATO's biggest military build-up on Russia's borders since the Cold War.

09 The withdrawal of international combat troops between 2011 and 2014 left a fragile security environment and a struggling national economy in Afghanistan. The Taliban is growing stronger with bold actions, which in turn contributes further to the instability at the center of Eurasia.

usually find their inspiration in 'rise-and-fall' realism. This stream of realism encompasses hegemonic transition theory (Gilpin, 1981), power transition theory (Organski, 1968; Organski & Kugler, 1980), and neo-classical realist theories (Schweller, 2011).

In a relatively crude way, the hegemonic transition theory of Gilpin focuses on how international order emerges from hegemonic wars, is shaped and sustained by dominant states, and how it comes under pressure from rising powers. Once there is a change in the distribution of power within the international system, the war over systemic leadership would then follow. This is mostly due to the states searching for possible ways to shape the system according to their preferences (Onderco, 2015).

The power transition perspective argues global politics is a hierarchy of nations with varying degrees of cooperation and competition. Consequently, it would be reasonable to say that this structural and dynamic approach focuses on the importance of status quo evaluations. Power transition centers on differential growth rates and their effect on modifying relative power between countries; producing new relationships among nations and the formation of new political/economic entities, which in turn illustrates how and why change occurs in the international system (Organski, 1968; Organski & Kugler, 1980). One expected outcome of this uneven growth is the significant potential for conflict when a challenger and a dominant nation attain the stage of relative equivalence of power, and specifically when the challenger is dissatisfied with the status quo (Onderco, 2015).

These two theories assume that rising powers are always revisionist. Such expectations are partially derived from the logic of offensive realism (Mearsheimer, 2001). Mearsheimer's theory of offensive realism can also be applied to the context of the rising regional power(s). Intriguingly, Mearsheimer's theory of offensive realism differs from Waltz's defensive realist theory (Waltz, 1979) not so much regarding the original assumptions but the conclusions. Mearsheimer concludes states will ceaselessly pursue power, while Waltz highlights how the balance-of-power inhibits power maximizing behavior and thus makes states satisfied, once they have adequate power. In the face of such uncertainty, the only policy option they can use is to maximize their security by maximizing their power (Mearsheimer, 2001).

It would be equally valuable to extend the scope of analysis of rising regional powers by including aspects such as culture, history, trade, religion, and civilization in the formation of national identity (Katzenstein, 1996; Lapid and Kratochwil, 1996). These influences would be especially pertinent in the study of 'rising powers,' where historical experience, culture, and civilization may have been greatly different from each other (Acharya & Buzan, 2007).

The research questions of this study are inherently exploratory and attempt to understand not only the origins of Iranian foreign policy, but also its possible trajectory in the coming decades. Hence, the chapter tries to reshapethe perceptions held on what/how different factors constrain/shape the Iranian foreign policy orientation, especially with regards to the Korean peninsula. In that aspect, the passage from unipolar to a multipolar global political structure plays a centripetal role in understanding this process of transformation.

After setting the parameters surrounding the quintessential characteristics of Iran, this study will provide a brief overview of Iranian foreign policy orientation from the Khatami period to the current Rouhani presidency. The subsequent sections will introduce the concept of Iran's 'Looking East' policy as a rising regional power contesting the legitimacy of the current international order (Gheissari, 2009; Pirzadeh, 2016). As for this uneasiness with the existing status quo, the article will finally try to shed some light on the Iranian foreign policy formulation towards the Korean peninsula.

Setting the Stage —

First and foremost, it is imperative to acknowledge Iran's fundamental geopolitical[10] importance. To a great extent, Iran is a

---

10 Geopolitics would be essential to the understanding of the behavior of human societies organized into complex, geographically well-defined systems. Evidently, in modern times, this approach translates itself to the study of nation-states. It would be fair to assert that geopolitics is the quest for the center of gravity of

natural bridge connecting Eurasia–from West to East and from North to South. However, in historical and cultural terms, considering Iran just as a bridge would be downplaying its prominent power, unrivaled importance, and majestic history.This in turn provides unequivocal self-confidence and firm determination when it comes to conducting foreign policy via the diplomatic chess games. Over the millenniums, Persia and Persian civilization demonstrated their capability to build a robust economy, conduct perplexing imperial politics, and manage vast territories containing various ethnicities throughout western and central Eurasia.

Several notable fortes might magnify Iran's importance further in global politics. For instance, Iran has the economic potential to be included in the G-20 countries due to its consistently high economic growth rates. In purchasing power parity (PPP) terms, it is already ranked eighteenth in the world. A dynamic and vibrant population of 80 million (approximately half being under age 35) is expected to reach 100 million by the mid-21st century. The influential Iranian diaspora living abroad such as the United States, Canada, Europe, Persian Gulf States, Turkey, Australia, and the broader Middle East represents a significant source of much needed foreign currency reserves through their remittances ("Remittance Flows Worldwide," 2016). Iran is also home

---

reality. Most certainly, the factors and actors at play are never entirely political, military or economic. For further details, see (Friedman, 2008).

to one of the largest refugee population in the world, mainly from two bordering countries, Afghanistan and Iraq. The global war on terror, the subsequent civil wars in those countries, and the geopolitical instability gave birth to a disastrous refugee situation in the region.[11]

Additionally, Iran is a natural energy resource giant with its full potential yet to realize (Kuhn, 2012). Globally, Iran possesses the fourth-largest proven oil reserves and the second-largest natural gas reserves.[12] Despite the country's extensive reserves, Iran's oil production has considerably declined, and natural gas production growth rates did not match government expectations ("Iran," 2015). Since the Revolution of 1979, internal divisions have left Iran vulnerable and mostly unable to benefit from its vast energy potentiality. International sanctions due to the fears of nuclear proliferation (Alexander & Hoeig, 2008; Bowen, Moran & Esfandiary, 2016; Gaietta, 2015; Jones, 2011; Kang, 2013; Onderco, 2015; Rezaei, 2017; Romashkina, 2007) took a heavy toll on Iran's energy realm by cancelling or delaying numerous prospective oil and gas projects.

In the 21st century, geography continues to be the source of some hefty geopolitical, environmental, and socio-economic conflicts, and Iran is

---

11 A decade of Soviet War in Afghanistan (1979-1989) had far-reaching consequences regarding the refugee situation in Iran, displacing up to six million people to neighboring Iran and Pakistan. Currently, Tehran shelters around one million registered and up to two million unregistered Afghans.

12 Iran also ranks among the globe's top ten oil producers and top five natural gas producers. Iran produced approximately 3.4 million barrels per day (b/d) of crude oil in 2014 and 5.7 trillion cubic feet (Tcf) of natural gas in 2013.

no exception to this. Iran lies at the center of many global geopolitical maneuvers such as the Strait of Hormuz.[13] Lying on the southeastern coast of Iran, it represents one of the most critical geopolitical maritime chokepoints, not just for Iran, but for all other Persian Gulf countries, too. The Strait is a must-go route and main artery for oil and natural gas shipments from all GCC countries, Iraq and Iran.

The Revolution of 1979 was also such a game changer in global politics that Iranian foreign policy has become a point of focus in western academic circles and has been subsequently studied extensively over the years (Beck, 2016; Katzman, 2017; Kinch, 2016; Murray, 2010; Offiler, 2015; Ryan, 2017; Warnaar, 2013). At the end of the Cold War, Samuel P. Huntington set forth an evolutionary theory "The Clash of Civilizations." He presents his work as a theory of culture and civilization that utilizes a modernization theory of political violence (Huntington, 1997). As such, it is also very much a geopolitical theory, since civilizations are in part defined by a specific, generally fixed territory. He

13 The Strait of Hormuz is a geo-strategically important strait connecting the Persian Gulf with the Arabian Sea (Indian Ocean). The Strait is only 33 to 95 km wide throughout its length. Iran and Oman are the countries surrounding the Strait of Hormuz and share territorial rights over its waters. Nearly 17 million b/d of crude oil and refined products passed through the Strait in 2013 (about 30% of all seaborne traded oil and 20% of the total oil produced globally). A substantial amount of another fossil fuel, liquefied natural gas (LNG) also moved through the Strait of Hormuz. Around 3.7 trillion cubic feet (Tcf) of LNG was transported from Qatar via the Strait of Hormuz in 2013, corresponding to more than 30% of global LNG trade.

hypothesizes conflict in the post-Cold War era will be between different cultures or civilizations, instead of ideologies. He argues this conflict will develop along cultural fault lines separating these civilizations from one another and equally predicts a likely clash between Western and Islamic civilization.

In simple terms, the theory of the clash of civilizations ought to take place between the liberal West and nearly all of the rest of the world, but especially the Islamic world. Cultural differences carved by religious norms would be instrumental in the creation of global fault lines separating those cultures. This insertion of 'religion as a norm' in international politics, combined with the impression of Islam as the liberal Western world's principal adversary, took a toll on some Islamic countries antagonistic to the West. But maybe, more importantly, the situation dangerously evolved with the coup de grace initiated by September 11 terrorist attacks in the United States (Hunter, 2010). To some extent, through the September 11 event, the clash of civilizations paradigm reestablished itself as a plausible explanatory power for international relations in the coming age of transformations. In that regard, the strategy of global war on terror was just a policy tool to handle an evolving struggle with the Muslim world.

Persian Culture and Identity —

Iranian people take pride in their cultural identity, and the civilizational values developed over three millenniums, which gave birth to an unequivocal and passionate sense of independence and a culture of resistance to foreign domination (Sharafedin, 2016). Consequently, analyzing Persian culture and civilization[14] is crucial to better understanding, not only Iranian foreign policy orientation, but also Iranian national characteristics.

Since the Islamic Revolution of 1979, the Western world has displayed, with saddening unity, a distorted representation of Iran, portraying it as a hysterical population of Islamic fanaticism and downplaying the actual cultural identity of Iranians. This distorted reality does not take into consideration that whilst the Iranians are very fond of their Islamic 'peculiarities', they are also equally receptive and appreciative of their pre-Islamic Persian identity. Many significant aspects of Iranian culture such as the infamous epic of Cyrus the Great,[15] the symbols of

14 In this study, civilization is acknowledged as a comprehensive term that represents the cumulative intellectuals, culture, and social achievements that have evolved over a considerable period and whose norms are practiced by a group of people.

15 Cyrus II of Persia was a 6th-century BCE iconic founder of the Achaemenid Empire, and in modern times revived as the embodiment of Persian nationalism and civilization.

the ancient Zoroastrians, the outstanding literary figures such as Abu'l-Qasim Ferdowsi Tusi,[16] Omar Khayyam,[17] and Hafez-e Shirazi[18] are genuinely embedded in the society's collective consciousness. Holidays and celebrations like Nowruz[19] and Charsanba-Suri[20] with considerable historical implications serve as a bridge connecting the ancient traditions to the present-day modern Iran.

---

16 Abu 'l-Qasim Ferdowsi Tusi was a 10th-century Persian poet and the author of the splendid Shahnameh (the most popular/influential national epic in Iran and the world's longest epic poem conceived by a single poet). He belonged to a class of landowning Iranian aristocrats called dehqan, which is intensely patriotic to preserve the Persian language and the cultural traditions.

17 Omar Khayyam was a 12th-century Persian mathematician, astronomer, and poet, notable for his work on cubic equations and his calendar reform. He moved from Nishapur (Seljuqi capital of its times and an influential religious center of Zoroastrians) in northeastern Iran where he was born, to first Samarkand then to Bukhara (currently Uzbekistan) to pursue his education. His calendar 'Al-Tarikh-al-Jalali' is much more precise than the Gregorian calendar and is to the point within one day in 3,770 years. Most importantly, he measured the length of the year as 365.24219858156 days, accurate to eleven decimal places.

18 Khwaja Shams-ud-Din Muhammad Hafez-e Shirazi is also known by his penname Hafez (the memorizer) or Hafiz and was a 14th-century remarkable literary figure who focused on currently controversial themes in Iran such as love, eroticism, wine, and religious hypocrisy. His masterpieces considered as a pinnacle of Persian poetry. Most certainly, Hafiz's verses did have an enduring influence on the people of Iran up to the modern epoch. It is inconceivable to dismiss the very-consequential impact of his work on the society. To a certain extent, Hafiz considered as the manifestation and awakening of Iran's national spirit through his literary work. For further information, see (Solati, 2015).

19 Nowruz (literally meaning "New Day") is the Iranian New Year containing religious Zoroastrian origins, celebrated by people from distinct ethnolinguistic communities in Western Asia, Central Asia, the Caucasus and the Black Sea Basin for over 3,000 years.

20 Charsanba-Suri is known as the Persian Festival of Fire and translated as the Red Wednesday. It is celebrated on the eve of the last Wednesday preceding Nowruz (the Iranian New Year) by displaying a ceremonial jumping over the fire. The origin of the festival traced back to at least 1,700 BCE, during the early Zoroastrian era.

The Safavids dynasty (1501-1722) instituted the origins of the modern state of Persia, forging a strong sense of cultural and religious identification by adopting the Twelver Shiite as the official religion. Due to Anglo-Russian rivalry in Central Asia throughout the Great Game in the second half of the 19th century, Persia was subject to interferences from Russia and the Great Britain. The fragile Qajar dynasty (1789 – 1925) was weakened further by these external threats and unable to create a strong opposition against them. Since the 19th century, the concept of Iranian identity has shifted to embrace nationalism and Islamism simultaneously or sometimes alternatively. Since then, Iran attempted to modernize and secularize during the Pahlavi dynasty (1925 – 1979), manufacturing an identity by beautifying the ancient symbols of the old Persia.

Islamic Revolution of 1979 —

The Revolution of 1979 was a mass movement with the intent of establishing a new political regime by violently transforming the existing government. The Iranian Revolution concluded the monarchy of Shah Mohammed Reza Pahlavi[21] and replaced it with an Islamic republic, the theocracy of Ayatollah Khomeini. The Revolution gave birth to a new Iran grounded on strict Islamic laws, exporting its revolutionary ideology and dismissing western civilizational values altogether.

The Iranian Shia theocracy had an eroding effect on neighboring countries with significant Shia populations.[22] For instance, Iraq felt particularly vulnerable and invaded Iran in 1980. The invasion was an attempt to prevent a possible Shia effort from taking over the Sunni-controlled government of Iraq. A disastrous eight-year war between Iran and Iraq had a catastrophic impact on Iran, although simultaneously it created a national solidarity movement opposing this external threat. Iraq was mainly supported by the United States and most Sunni Arab regimes such as Saudi Arabia. Consequently, Iranians forged an adverse perception of the United States and Gulf Cooperation Council (GCC) countries,[23] which affected its future relationship with them.

---

21 The Pahlavi dynasty (1925-1979) replaced the Qajar dynasty (1789-1925).

22 The Shia majority countries are Iraq, Azerbaijan, and Bahrain. Shias constitute 30% of the population in Lebanon, over 35 % of the population in Yemen, 30%-35% of the citizen population in Kuwait, over 20% in Turkey, 5–20% of the population in Pakistan, 10-19% of Afghanistan's population, and 15% of the local population in Saudi Arabia. Significant Shia communities exist in the coastal regions of West Sumatra and Aceh in Indonesia.

23 Gulf Cooperation Council (May 25, 1981) is a loose regional intergovernmental political and economic union consisting of all Arab states of the Persian Gulf, except Iraq. It was founded in 1981 against the backdrop of the Islamic Revolution in Iran. The member states of GCC are Bahrain, Kuwait, Oman, Qatar, Saudi

According to the central tenets of the Iranian constitution, in the aftermath of the Islamic Revolution, the country's foreign policy orientation was crafted according to a few fundamental principles. First and foremost, the rejection of all forms of external domination was coined to firmly preserve Iran's absolute independence and territorial integrity. The constitution also distinctively emphasized the rights of all Muslims without allying with hegemonic powers and the maintenance of peaceful relations with all non-aggressive states.

These principles became the cornerstone of Iranian foreign policy since. Nevertheless, a pragmatic approach has been adopted by decision-makers in Iran, and this tends to be driven by regional and international developments. In the light of these principles, it is easy to understand the Islamic Republic's foreign policy and its support for Islamic resistance movements around the world. Also, they further clarify the so-called concept of 'exporting the revolution', extensively promoted by many of those decision-makers in the 1980s ("Iran," 2015).

It is possible to argue Iran's aspirations to depict itself as the heart of the Muslim world are a bid to gain universal Muslim support, which provides to Iran more legitimacy in disregarding regional and global challenges. However, the above-mentioned principles guiding Iranian foreign policy have created 'enemies of Islam and Iran' as the

---

Arabia, and the United Arab Emirates.

Islamic Republic regards the West in general and the United States in particular as enemies (Solati, 2015). This animosity has led to the current confrontation between Iran and Western powers because the United States and some European countries consider Iran and its foreign policy the greatest threat to security and stability in the region. At crucial junctures, this animosity has tended to dominate Iran's relations with the West. There is a broadly held belief among Iranians that the backing Iraq received from the West throughout the Iran–Iraq war in the 1980s was due to the Islamic nature of the Iranian regime.

In this context, it is not too difficult to understand why Iranians have tried to shift their partnerships towards the East. Current political setting is the outcome of cultural attacks on the main principles of the Islamic revolution. The infamous British and American interventionist policies in Iran during the 20th century, such as the US-backed overthrow of Prime Minister Muhammad Musaddiq, is a solid case to illustrate this trend.[24]

The majority of Iranian politicians believe that moving towards the East is less risky than building relations with the West, with its hegemonic tendencies. Thus, Iran considers China a model to follow. Leading figures in the Iranian political system, Khamenei, Rafsanjani,

---

24 The United States aborted Iranian democratic aspirations in 1953 by overthrowing the government of Prime Minister Muhammad Musaddiq, returned the autocratic Shah to the throne, and thereafter dominated the country for a quarter century is deeply seared into Iran's collective memory.

and Ahmadinejad, have all showed similar convictions.

Furthermore, Iran has also rapidly moved towards other parts of the world such as Latin America and Africa. Respective Iranian governments built resilient relations with the developing Global South,[25] including Brazil, Cuba, and Venezuela. Through this, Iranian policy-makers are not only aiming to strengthen the economy but also trying to alleviate the pressures put on them by the West and the United States.

Foreign Policy Orientation of Iran: From Khatami to Rouhani —

Iranian foreign policy decision-making process seems very complex and sophisticated, reflecting the peculiarities of the institutional setting. The Iranian political elite can be divided into four main groups: classics, conservatives, reformists, and neoconservatives. Almost all Iranian politicians, except for a group of reformists, agree on the principles highlighted by the Islamic Revolution. That particular

25 The Global South is made up of Africa, Latin America, and developing Asia including the Middle East which largely corresponds with the Third World (three quarters of the world populations but having access to one-fifth of the world income).

group believes it is necessary to maintain relations with the West, arguing Iranian foreign policy is distorting Iran's image. For this reason, they call for a serious review of Iranian foreign policy.

Over the eight years that preceded Ahmadinejad's coming to power in 2005, Muhammad Khatami's foreign policy was shaped by twin objectives: firstly, to create close connections between domestic agenda and foreign policy issues, and secondly, to improve Iran's relations with the world through a policy of détente and mutual respect.

To a certain extent, Khatami was successful in improving the image of both the ayatollahs and Iran. This new, positive impression of the Islamic Republic helped it to gain a more prominent status and play a more influential role in the Middle East and beyond. By 2001, Khatami's initiative, the Dialogue among Civilizations, bestowed much respect upon Iran and its president. The new, relaxed atmosphere helped replace the prevailing belief that Iranian foreign policy was 'closely' connected to – and indeed an extension of – policies and priorities of the theocratic regime and its dominant elite (Ehteshami & Zweiri, 2008).

This 'radical change' in the direction of Iranian foreign policy under Khatami presidency had a profound impact on Iran's relations with some European countries in particular, such as France, Spain, Greece, and Italy. Khatami became the first Iranian president who officially visited those countries since the 1979 revolution.

The ninth presidential election in June 2005 brought to power a new Iranian leadership that did not follow in the footsteps of Khatami.

Mahmoud Ahmadinejad vigorously pursued the Eastern shift and the Third World-first policies originally articulated in the 1980s. He also revived the fiery rhetoric against Israel and launched a major campaign of Holocaust denial, the views that had almost completely disappeared during Khatami's presidency (Ehteshami & Zweiri, 2008).

Iranian foreign policy under Ahmadinejad presidency proved to be a constant source of tension on both regional and international levels. The unexpected political developments on the domestic level affected Iran's foreign policy and regional relations. Whilst some may question Ahmadinejad's foreign policy decision-making process, its complexity and the relationship amongst power centers can lead to misunderstanding the Iranian political system (Warnaar, 2013).

Although Ahmadinejad had administrative power to pursue Iran's relations with the remaining parts of the world, this jurisdiction was still limited. This limitation of authority in the international arena revealed itself when Ayatollah Khamenei appointed Dr. Kamal Kharrazi, former foreign affairs minister, as the head of a new foreign policy advisory committee, which is accountable directly to the Supreme Leader's office, not to the president (Warnaar, 2013).

President Hassan Rouhani then became the seventh president of the Islamic Republic of Iran in 2013. Rouhani's campaign advocated moderation, promised a government of prudence and hope, and raised expectations of a looming change in Iran's international engagement (Beck, 2016).

A combination of Rouhani's significant credentials, international reputation, and the scale of his popular mandate gave him substantial political capital. Rouhani articulated an aspiring strategy for the foreign policy reform based on three pillars: rebuilding the economy, resolving the nuclear issue, and ending Iran's international isolation. There is no doubt that after the tumultuous years of Ahmadinejad's leadership, rebuilding the Iranian economy was Rouhani's priority. However, this would also vehemently require dismantling the international sanctions imposed on Iran. President Rouhani indicated the scale of those ambitions by proclaiming Iran's economic potential to be among the world's top ten within three decades. On the other hand, Iran's nuclear ambitions and the question of a clandestine nuclear weapons program have always been a point of frustration between Iran and the international community. Upon election, Rouhani quickly moved to negotiate the nuclear issue and commit Iran to the interim agreement in November 2013 (Beck, 2016).

Looking East —

Iran's strategy of expanding economic and other relations with some key Asian countries is an effort to circumvent the

Western nations' mounting economic and political pressures. Apparently, Iran's economic needs and its desire to escape international isolation have partly motivated this strategy. Of unwillingness to accept the emerging post-Soviet international system (based on U.S./Western hegemony), Iran has tried to create a multipolar world by forming an alliance with other countries to counterweight Western powers.

There is also a coherent rationale behind the Iranian desire to investigate opportunities in the Far East. First and foremost, historically, Iran has been dismissed mostly by the Arabian Middle East because of its Persian and Shia character. Furthermore, after the disintegration of the Soviet Union,[26] Iran has faced the challenging Pan-Turkic movements in Central Asia. Although from a historical point of view Iran and Central Asia had always been vigorously engaged with each other on cultural, commercial, and political grounds. After the breakup of the USSR, this region was not a priority for the Iranian foreign policy. However, increasing ethnocentricity levels in Turkmenistan and Azerbaijan (both Turkic states) concerned Iranian foreign policymakers as Iran itself is home to many Turkmen and Azeri minority groups. Conversely, Western powers' farfetched anxiety of Iran exporting its Islamic revolution to

---

26 In December 1991, five new states—Kazakhstan, Kyrgyzstan, Tajikistan, Turkmenistan, and Uzbekistan—emerged in Central Asia from the ashes of the Soviet empire. In modern times, these five countries have never enjoyed the status of independent actors in the international arena. Consequently, this remarkable increase of independent states at the heart of Eurasia gave rise to a number of convoluted political, legal, environmental, and economic problems.

Central Asia and Caucasus proved to be unsubstantiated. All of the newly independent Soviet Central Asian states belong to Sunni branch of Islam, not Shia like in Iran.[27]

Consequently, Iran hoped the development of a Pan-Asian identity, and movement toward intra-Asian cooperation (and even eventually the Asian Union) would alleviate its ethnic, religious, and cultural isolation. Iran, like many other countries, considers the 21st century the "Asian Century." Subsequently, their policymakers' roadmap stresses further possible rapprochement with the Far East. The mega-infrastructure and logistics development projects, highlighted by China's One Belt One Road (OBOR)[28] initiative, would inherently create a long-searched foreign policy overture for Iran.

In that regard, Iran considers China as a strategic partner due to China's rise and its subsequent eminence in global politics (Erdem, 2015, 2016). Iran is remarkably relevant regarding Chinese energy security due to Iran's geographic location. Moreover, Iran, a leading

---

27 Tajiks are the only ethnicity in Soviet Central Asia representing a wide range of Persian-speaking people of Iranian origin (located in Tajikistan, Afghanistan, and Uzbekistan). However, they are overwhelmingly Sunni, which makes difficult for Iran to assert itself through politics based on religious identity. Azerbaijan is the only country that belongs to Shia branch of Islam, but Azeri is pertain to Turkic linguistic and ethnic family.

28 OBOR is considered the most substantial overseas investment project initiated by a single country. China is planning to invest up to $900bn in infrastructure projects, ranging from ports to high-speed railways to gas pipelines to increase Chinese access to those markets. For further information, see (Hancock, 2017).

power in the unstable energy-rich Middle East, is not an ally of the US. China was a major consumer of Iranian oil even throughout the years of international sanctions targeting Iran's nuclear program. China has also been Iran's most significant trading partner for the past decade or so. After the termination of the sanctions against Iran, it is expected the trade volume between them show impressive growth rates, reaching new all-time highs; Chinese President Xi Jinping's 2016 visit to President Hassan Rouhani in Tehran highlighted a mutual desire to increase trade volumes up to US$600 billion within a decade (Sharafedin, 2016). In addition to China's energy security issue, Iran will also play a pivotal role in China's pursuit of its OBOR, massive infrastructure development projects connecting China to the rest of Eurasia.

Iran's Relations with South Korea —

Despite ideological differences and different alliances, Iran has retained a reasonable relationship with non-Muslim Asian countries, notably South Korea. Iran's attraction to South Korea derives from the following factors: Iran's vast oil and gas reserves and substantial markets. Iran has also maintained reasonable relations with South Korea throughout the 1980s, despite ideological differences and Iran's close ties with North Korea. In 1987, there were approximately 2,000 South Korean nationals working in various projects in Iran. Following the end of the war in Iraq and the start of the period of reconstruction, Iran also hoped to enlist South Korea in its rebuilding activities (Hunter, 2010).

For most of the 1990s, however, Iran's economic relations with South Korea were limited to trade. From 2000 and onwards, South Korea began investing in Iran, mostly in the energy sector. A significant event in the evolution of the Iran–South Korea relations was the visit of the South Korean Minister of Foreign Affairs, Hang Seung Soo, to Tehran in August 2001. During this trip, he met with President Khatami, who said this trip marked a new chapter in the two countries' relations, calling for greater South Korean investment in Iran. The relationship hit a snag in 2003 when South Korea supported the decision of International Atomic Energy Agency (IAEA) to reprimand Iran for not meeting the UN's demands. It prompted Iran's foreign minister, Kamal Kharazi, to say "the Islamic Republic of Iran will pay attention to balancing economic cooperation with political ties in its relations with other countries." In 2005, the relationship hit another low point when South Korea voted in the IAEA to refer Iran's nuclear record to the United Nations Security Council, leading Iranian authorities to indicate they might ban the import of South Korean goods. However, the efforts by South Korea, along with Iran's economic and investment needs, prevented a rupture in the relationship (Hunter, 2010).

In February 2005, the head of South Korea's Chamber of Commerce visited Iran to discuss ways to improve trade and investment conditions for Korean businesspeople in Iran. In 2007, the two countries signed an agreement, according to which South Korea will invest US$500 million in an LNG project for the gas in South Pars, and in 2008 they established a joint investment committee. In October 2009, Iran's Mehr News Agency reported Iran and South Korea's GS Holdings signed a new agreement for the development of Iran's Pars gas field, worth 1.2 billion euros. In short, Iran retained its commercial relations with South Korea although these relations would have been much higher in the absence of political irritants (Hunter, 2010).

In recent years, Iran's primary interest in South Korea has been to expand the commercial relationship and weaken the impact of the US sanctions. There is no doubt the United States' opposition has also limited the scope of South Korea's economic ties with Iran. Although South Korea has not been heavily involved in security and strategic issues in the Middle East, the country remains a close ally of the United States, and their firms have been consistently unwilling to risk their positions in the U.S. market by violating any U.S. sanctions on Iran. Moreover, the international weight and influence of the United States, plus the extensive and complicated economic, trade, and financial relations between America and South Korea, have played a significant role in South Korea's decision to curtail its military ties to Iran. South Korea is also wary of Iran's military and technology relations with North Korea (Kang, 2013). Economic links between Iran and South Korea, mainly oil purchases, are improving; now the international sanctions have eased out (Katzman, 2017).

South Korea's President Park Geun-Hye visited Tehran in May 2016. For the first time since 1962, a South Korean president had been in Iran in the company of 236 South Korean businesspeople. The two sides signed many agreements on the domains of energy, railways, tourism, and technology, and agreed to re-establish direct flights between their respective capitals, Tehran and Seoul (Katzman, 2017).

It is important to remember Iranian 'Looking East' policy is also reciprocal. For instance, South Korea's New Eurasia initiative also intends to integrate the entirety of Eurasia. In 2013, the President of South Korea, Park Geun-Hye, proposed the "Eurasia Initiative." Under the motto of "one continent, creative continent, and peaceful continent," this ambitious proposal aimed to develop a unified system of transport, energy, and trade networks across the vast Eurasian continent. The ultimate goal is the gradual elimination of all trade barriers, leading to the establishment of broad free trade zones. The main geopolitical aim of this strategic move by South Korea is to align itself with China's OBOR strategy. Correspondingly, linking energy and logistics infrastructures through Eurasian transport corridors is expected to diminish the tensions with North Korea which will be incorporated into a multilateral negotiation process (Kim, 2015).

Iran's Relations with North Korea —

Since the Democratic People's Republic of Korea (DPRK) was founded in 1948, the country's defense policy has focused on maintaining and extending its military might and offensive potential in the region. Moreover, the security situation on the Korean peninsula has not decreased over the years after the Korean War (1950-1953) and during the Cold War period. Interestingly, the Islamic Republic of Iran's relations with DPRK, which were close in the 1980s, has stagnated after the collapse of the Soviet Union. To a great extent, this situation arose due to Iran's needs and North Korea's economic shortcomings (Hunter, 2010).

Iran and North Korea have been aligned as fellow "rogue states" subjugated to extensive international sanctions. North Korea is one of the few countries Iran has formal military relations with, and the two countries have collaborated on a broad range of military and Weapons of Mass Destruction (WMD)-related endeavors, particularly the advancement of ballistic missile technology. Previously, Iran reportedly funded and assisted in the re-transfer of missile and possibly nuclear technology from North Korea to Syria. North Korea also supplied Iran with small but capable submarines (Katzman, 2017).

North Korea did not commit to abide by international sanctions against Iran, but its economy is too small to help Iran significantly. Some observers claim a portion of China's oil purchases from Iran and other suppliers are re-exported to North Korea. However, now international sanctions on Iran's crude oil exports have been removed, and it is likely that additional quantities of Iranian oil are reaching North Korea, probably via China (Katzman, 2017).

The DPRK-Iran cooperation vis-à-vis ballistic missile program dates back to the 1980s when Iran acquired Scud B and C Short Range Ballistic Missiles (SRBMs) and the factory to build them from the DPRK. Iran called these missiles Shahab[29] 1 and 2. Evidently, this relationship continued in the early 1990s with Iran reportedly providing some funding to the DPRK to develop the Medium Range Ballistic Missile (MRBM), which the West identifies as the Nodong 1 (Offiler, 2015).

Recently, North Korea modified and sold Soviet missile technology to Iran. However, Iran's development of a more advanced sizeable and robust rocket motor program for a long-range missile (probably an Intercontinental Ballistic Missile (ICBM)) with North Korean involvement indicates some technology transfer has reversed(Offiler, 2015).

Nonetheless, in the past decade or so, some critical developments occurred regarding North Korean and Iranian long-range ballistic missile

29 The DPRK calls these Hwasong 5 and 6, respectively.

programs such as the development of North Korea's Nodong 2 and Iran's Shahab 3M with a common tri-conic reentry vehicle. North Korea purchased from the Russian Federation the SS-N-6 based Musudan/BM-25 Intermediate Range Submarine Launched Ballistic Missile (IR-SLBM) and sold 18 of these to Iran. Some speculated both countries have a kind of ICBM development program and are working together.

As North Korea firmly resumes its march towards developing a reliable long-range nuclear missile, the world is also showing some serious concerns over the DPRK's ties to Iran. Some countries, particularly the United States, exhibit anxiety while the DPRK improves its nuclear and missile capabilities, fearing this knowledge and technology could be shared if approached by potential customers such as Iran (Cohen, 2017). The three-decade long cooperative missile partnership between Iran and North Korea was favorable to both sides: Iran providing the money to purchase weapons and manufacturing capabilities, which in turn enables North Korea to build its own missile forces (Offiler, 2015).

Conclusion —

Iran as an emerging regional power in global politics would seriously challenge the current status quo and Western interests in the Middle East. The long-delayed but expected rise should be welcomed and may be just a normal and healthy political outcome, given the rapid and substantial global transformations taking place in recent decades. Although it may seem peculiar at the moment, it can lead to a more stable relation with the Middle East and Central Eurasia over the long run.

There are already some credible signs indicating an evolution in that direction—advances in space technology, emerging cyber-power, progress in military hardware production, as well as a large and educated population. Moreover, the Islamic Republic of Iran can project power and influence effectively in adjacent geographical areas in the Middle East such as Yemen, the Levant, and the Gulf or Central Asia such as Afghanistan and those newly acquired capabilities challenging the United States. Additionally, the usual geopolitical realities provide more muscle to Iranian status as a rising regional power. Needless to say, the strategic control over the Strait of Hormuz, the coastline on the Caspian Sea, as well as significant oil and gas reserves all contribute and solidify Iran's claim for a major power role in the Middle East.

However, current Iranian political engagements in the near abroad in order to influence and/or defend its interests may encounter severe limitations. The primary tool of Iran's foreign policy was the sectarian Shia politics; however, Shias constitute a modest minority in the Muslim world. Too many factional politics may deteriorate Iran's relations with Sunni-majority countries such as Indonesia, Malaysia, Bangladesh, and Pakistan. Consequently, from a 'Looking East' perspective, the diplomatic and economic relations with non-Muslim Asia can provide a substantial leverage to its rising regional power status.

The Korean peninsula in general and South Korea in particular would be instrumental in achieving the regime's goals mentioned earlier. Simultaneously, South Korea develops a growing appetite for Middle Eastern oil, as well as a penchant to compete with other countries for very profitable business deals in the region. With a vibrant young and educated population, the Islamic Republic of Iran offers tremendous economic and commercial potential for South Korean businesses to flourish in those markets.

Although much remains to be done, this study mainly focused on Iranian foreign policy fundamentals and the strategic concept of 'Looking East.' It was not in the scope of this study to provide an extended discussion on the possible impacts of China's OBOR initiative. However, this study would benefit substantially by extending the analysis in that direction. The investigation of the potential benefits and the drawbacks of OBOR would be only complementary to the current study by providing a better understanding of the big picture.

References —

Acharya, A.,& Buzan, B. (2007). Why is there no non-Western international relations theory? An introduction. *International Relations of the Asia-Pacific, 7*(3), 287–312.

Alexander, Y,. & Hoeig, M. (2008). *The New Iranian leadership: Ahmadinejad, terrorism, nuclear ambition, and the Middle East.* Westport, CT: Praeger Security International.

Beck, L. (Ed.). (2016). *Iranian foreign policy context: Regional analyses and U.S. interests.* New York: Nova Publishers.

Bowen, W., Moran, M., & Esfandiary, D. (2016). *Living on the edge: Iran and the practice of nuclear hedging.* London: Palgrave Macmillan.

Cohen, Z. (2017). Could North Korea help Iran develop nuclear weapons? *CNN.* Retrieved from http://edition.cnn.com/2017/09/14/politics/north-korea-iran-nuclear-weapons-program/index.html website:

Ehteshami, A., & Zweiri, M. (Eds.) (2008). *Iran's foreign policy: From Khatami to Ahmadinejad.* Berkshire, UK: Ithaca Press.

Erdem, C. (2015). Sino-Russian strategic partnership: the Shanghai Cooperation Organization. In E. Sorhun, Ü. Hacıoğlu & H. Dinçer (Eds.). *Regional economic integration and the global financial system* (pp. 257-273). Hershey, PA: IGI Global.

Erdem, C. (2016). The Eurasian corridor through the new Silk

Road: Differing geopolitical perceptions. *Acta Via Serica, Winter(Inaugural)*, 51-69.

Friedman, G. (2008). *The methodology of geopolitics: Love of one's own and the importance of place*. Austin, TX: Stratfor.

Gaietta, M. (2015). *The trajectory of Iran's nuclear program*. New York: Palgrave Macmillan.

Gheissari, A. (Ed.). (2009). *Contemporary Iran : Economy, society, politics*. New York, NY: Oxford University Press.

Gilpin, R. (1981). *War and change in world politics*. Cambridge: Cambridge University Press.

Hancock, T. (2017). China encircles the world with One Belt, One Road strategy. *Financial Times, May 4*. Retrieved from https://www.ft.com/content/0714074a-0334-11e7-aa5b-6bb07f5c8e12 website:

Hunter, S. T. (2010). *Iran's foreign policy in the post-Soviet era: Resisting the new international order*. Santa Barbara, California: Praeger.

Huntington, Samuel P. (1997). *The clash of civilizations and the remaking of world order*. New Delhi, India: Peguine Books.

Iran. (2015). *Energy information administration (EIA)*. Retrieved from https://www.eia.gov/beta/international/country.cfm?iso=IRN website:

Jones, J. (2011). *The American rhetorical construction of the Iranian nuclear threat*. London: Continuum International Publishing Group.

Kang, J. (Ed.). (2013). *Assessment of the nuclear programs of Iran and North*

Korea. New York, NY: Springer.

Katzenstein, P. J. (Ed.). (1996). *The culture of national security: Norms and identity in world politics*. New York: Columbia University Press.

Katzman, K. (2017). *Iran's foreign and defense policies*. Washington, DC: Congressional Research Service.

Kim, T. (2015). Beyond geopolitics: South Korea's Eurasia Initiative as a new nordpolitik. *The Asian Forum, 4*(4). February 16.

Kinch, P. (2016). *The US-Iran relationship: The impact of political identity on foreign policy*. London: I. B. Tauris.

Kuhn, M. (2012). *Enabling the Iranian gas export options: The destiny of Iranian energy relations in a tripolar struggle over energy security and geopolitics*. Berlin: Springer.

Lapid, Y., & Kratochwil, F. V. (Eds.). (1996). *The return of culture and identity in IR theory*. Boulder, CO: Lynne Rienner.

Mearsheimer, J. J. (2001). *The tragedy of great power politics*. New York: W.W. Norton.

Murray, D. (2010). *US foreign policy and Iran: American–Iranian relations since the Islamic Revolution*. New York: Routledge.

Offiler, B. (2015). *US foreign policy and the modernization of Iran: Kennedy, Johnson, Nixon, and the Shah*. New York, NY: Palgrave Macmillan.

Onderco, M. (2015). *Iran's nuclear program and the Global South: The foreign policy of India, Brazil, and South Africa*. New York, NY: Palgrave Macmillan.

Organski, A. F. K. (1968). *World politics*. New York: Knopf.

Organski, A. F. K., & Kugler, J. (1980). *The war ledger*. Chicago: University of Chicago Press.

Pirzadeh, A. (2016). *Iran revisited: Exploring the historical roots of culture, economics, and society*. Switzerland: Springer International Publishing.

Remittance Flows Worldwide. (2016). Retrieved from http://www.pewglobal.org/interactives/remittance-map/ website:

Rezaei, F. (2017). *Iran's nuclear program: A study in proliferation and rollback*. London: Palgrave Macmillan.

Romashkina, N. P. (2007). North Korea and Iran's nuclear programs as instability factors in the new system of international relations. *The Marshall Center Occasional Paper Series*, 13. Garmisch-Partenkirchen: The George C. Marshall European Center for Security Studies.

Ryan, G. (2017). *US foreign policy towards China, Cuba and Iran: The politics of recognition*. New York: Routledge.

Schweller, R. L. (2011). Emerging powers in an age of disorder. *Global Governance*, 17(3), 285–297.

Sharafedin, B. (2016). Iran's leader says never trusted the West, seeks closer ties with China. Retrieved from https://www.reuters.com/article/us-iran-china/irans-leader-says-never-trusted-the-west-seeks-closer-ties-with-china-idUSKCN0V109V website:

Solati, B. (2015). Hafiz and the Persians. Retrieved from http://www.

iranchamber.com/literature/articles/hafiz_and_the_persians.pdf website:

Waltz, K. N. (1979). *Theory of international politics*. Reading, MA: Addison-Wesley.

Warnaar, M. (2013). *Iranian foreign policy during Ahmadinejad: Ideology and actions*. New York, NY: Palgrave Macmillan.

Iran in the Changing World: Outsiders' Perspective

II

The Korea-Iran Relation in Trade and Foreign Direct Investment: A Review of the Past for the Future

Jung Soo Seo, Keimyung University

Ⅱ

The Korea-Iran Relation in Trade and Foreign Direct Investment: A Review of the Past for the Future

Jung Soo Seo

Abstract —

Korea and Iran had developed a bilateral relationship in history although the recent development has begun with the diplomatic tie established in 1962. The year 1962 has coincided with the Korea's First Five Year Economic Development plan. Korea has achieved a rapid economic expansion during the 1962-2016. Among many factors, exports and imports have played significant roles for Korea's economic development. By reviewing the development of Korea's trade, the evolution of Korea's trade structure has been highlighted. Similarly, by expounding briefly the bilateral trade relationship between Korea and Iran, their mutually complementing economic and production structures, as reflected in the trade structure, have been emphasized. By discussing Korea's OFDI trend and its sectoral distribution, this study observed Iran has been an outlier for Korea's OFDI. Thus, it suggests that Korean firms and businesses need to be ready to recoup the benefits accruing from the Iranian economic projections in the post-sanctions relief period through FDI and trade.

Keywords
Korea, Iran, Trade, FDI, Maritime Silk Road

Introduction —

The Islamic Republic of Iran (Iran, henceforth) is a country of long history and a large country in terms of territory, population, economy, and natural resource endowments, particularly in the Middle East and North Africa (MENA) region. Iran occupies apporximately1.65 million km^2 of territory, the seventeenth largest in the world and the fifth largest in the MENA region, after Algeria, Saudi Arabia, Sudan, and Libya. In terms of population, Iran has over 80 million inhabitants, as of May 2017, the second largest in the region, only after Egypt that has almost 93 million in the same year. Among this populace in Iran, according to the CIA's World Factbook, approximately 71% are economically active population, aged between 15 and 64, while those who are 65 and older account for 5.4% of the total population. As for the economy, according to the IMF's World Economic Outlook database, Iran's gross domestic product (GDP) in 2016 amounts to US$422.3 billion and is the second largest from the MENA region, after Saudi Arabia which has US$821.9 billion of GDP in the same year. So far as the natural endowments are concerned, additionally, Iran shows a distinctive feature, unlike Korea. In 2016 Iran's proven crude oil reserve amounts to 157.8 billion barrel, equivalent to the world's fourth largest, whilst the proven natural gas reserve is 34.02 trillion m^3, the second largest in the world (The World Factbook, 2017). As such, Iran's economic activity and government revenues still depend to a large extent on oil revenues and therefore remain volatile, subject to the international oil price fluctuations.

Iran adopted a comprehensive development strategy through market-based forms, in the name of five-year development plan when Iran has implemented its first five-year development plan in 1990, after the 1979 Islamic Revolution and with the ending of highly destructive eight-year-long war with Iraq (1980-1988). Currently, Iran is undertaking the sixth five-year economic development (2016-2020). Under the main pillars of economy, science and technology, and culture, the Iranian government envisages eight percent economic growth rate during the plan period.

Following the international decision to lift the economic and financial sanctions imposed on Iran on July 14, 2015 and the enforcement of the lifting sanction which has come into effect on January 14, 2016, the future of the Iran economy seems to augur well. In fact, the World Bank has dubbed relief from sanctions will be 'a windfall' for the Iranian economy (World Bank, 2015). However, it is warned that Iran will face several challenges in the post-sanction relief era. They will need to implement sound macroeconomic policies in order to benefit from the windfall whilst curbing the unwanted side effects associated with the so-called Dutch disease which may arise from Iran's access to international oil markets. Iran also has to ensure international investors in order to attract their investments in upgrading social and economic infrastructure and building capacities, particularly in oil and other resource extraction sectors.

Korea has a long historical relationship with Iran, also known as Persia, which stretches over more than a millennium ago. Recently, researchers have discovered Korea's relations with Iran would have dated back to Korea's Silla kingdom, as reflected in a Persia's ancient epic, the Kushnameh (refer to Lee (2011) and some references therein). They argued the bilateral relationship between Korea and Iran would have to be considered beyond economic and political spheres. In spite of such a long historical relationship, however, the modern day bilateral relations between them have commenced from when the two countries established a diplomatic tie on October 23, 1962 and more notably since the 1970s. The modern day relationship between them has developed predominantly in the scope of economy and trade. Thus, it will be timely to review Korea's bilateral relationship with Iran, in the context of exports and imports, as well as foreign direct investment in order to find measures to improve cooperation during the Iran's sanction relief era. In this context, the evolution of the bilateral relationship will be particularly highlighted.

The Role of Trade in Korea's Economic Development —

• Evolution of Korea's Trade

According to the International Monetary Fund (IMF), in 2016, Korea is the eleventh largest economy in the world in terms of GDP, and its GDP amounts to approximately US$1.521 trillion. As it has been well known to academics, researchers, and policy makers, this economic standing of Korea in 2016 is the outcome of its remarkable economic development achieved during the last half century since the early-1960s. After Korea has implemented its first five-year economic development plan in 1962, Korea has experienced leaps and bounds of growth. Korea's GDP, in the 2010 constant dollar term, has grown by more than 42 times, from approximately US$29.7 billion in 1962 to US$1,266.6 billion in 2015. This expansion is equivalent to the annual average growth rate of 7.1%,[30] as seen in Table 2-1. Paralleling the overall economic expansion, Korea's GDP per head has also remarkably increased: in fact, more than 22 folds, from US$1,118 in 1962 to US$25,022 in 2015, when measured in the 2010 constant dollar term.[31]

Table 2-1. Korea's Economic Growth Rates1, 1962-2015

Period	1962-1971	1972-1981	1982-1991	1992-1997	1998-2001	2002-2007	2008-2015
Average Growth Rate (%)	9.9	8.9	10.2	7.5	4.6	5.0	3.1

Note: 1. Compound average growth rates.
Source: The author's own calculation based on the World Bank World Development Indicators database.

Many factors have contributed to the Korea's economic success in the past half century. Among those factors, the roles played by Korea's trade, especially the exports, are undeniable. As many people have called Korea's economic development as an export-led development, export has been the engine of Korea's economic growth (Hong, 1987; Yoo, 2008). At the initial stage of export growth, the main thrust for Korea's

---

30 This is a compound average growth rates during the period 1962-2015.

31 This is equivalent to the compound average growth rate of 5.9% during the concerned period.

export expansion was fundamentally 'getting prices right' policies such as unification of exchange rates from the multiple to the single rate and subsequently won devaluations and depreciations (Kim, 1991). By getting prices right, nevertheless, resource allocations in Korea have improved. These policy measures were often accompanied by the states' selective interventions in the markets. At the same time, however, the Korean government has provided a variety of pecuniary and non-pecuniary incentives to businesses and companies in the export sector (Heo, 2001). These firms and businesses in the export industry have been exposed to competition in the world markets, which has, in turn, stimulated technological improvement and efficiency gains through technology transfer and/or their own R&D activities.

Over the period from 1962 to 2015, Korea's export growth rate was over 18% per year on average in the 2010 US dollar term, more than twice as fast as the GDP growth rate of 7.1% in the corresponding period. Similarly, the expansion of exports, and thus Korea's GDP expansion, has also accompanied the rapid expansion of imports, which has grown at the average rate of over 13.2% per annum in the same period (Table 2-2). The parallel increases of both export and import have well reflected the nature of Korea's deficient natural resource endowments such as petroleum, natural gas, coals, iron ores, etc. and also the capital goods like machineries, equipment, and intermediate products.

Table 2-2. Real Growth Rates[1] of Exports and Imports in Korea, 1962-2015

Period	Growth Rate of Exports (%, p.a.)	Growth Rate of Imports (%, p.a.)
1962-1971	29.5	20.7
1972-1981	21.2	14.2
1982-1991	11.2	12.0
1992-1997	15.3	12.4
1998-2001	10.3	2.7
2002-2007	13.3	11.6
2008-2015	5.6	4.2

Note: 1. Average compound growth rates during the respective period.
Source: The author's own calculation based on the World Bank World Development Indicators database.

As a result of the rapid expansion of both exports and imports, the trade ratio to GDP, commonly known as the openness of economy, has expanded rapidly too (Figure 2-1). Korea's openness stood only at 21% of the GDP in 1962 and increased to almost 70% by the early 1980s. However, the ratio generally showed a declining trend throughout the 1980s until it increased again from the early 1990s. At the dawn of the Asian financial crisis, the ratio hit approximately the 75% mark in 1998, as both exports and imports in Korea have grown fast. During the Asian financial crisis period, exports increased by more than 10%, import decreased by 24% in 1998 and managed to increase during the period by 2.7%.

The export expansion during the crisis period was attributed to the boosted international price competitiveness, subsequent to the plummeting Korean won. The average exchange rate of Korean won per US dollar on a year-on-year basis increased by more than 18% in 1997 and further soared by more than 47% in 1998. The imports decreased for the symmetric reason, and it was further combined with the contracted domestic demand in Korea during the crisis period. As such, the overall openness ratio has declined. Although the ratio bounced back briefly in 1999, it continued falling until 2002 when the ratio reached the 60% mark. The main reason was associated with the global economic contraction following the dot.com bubble burst that caused the stock market crash. From 2003, however, Korea's openness ratio increased rapidly, and the ratio reached 110% in 2010, the highest ratio, except the global financial crisis (GFC) period of 2008-2009.

But in the post-GFC period, the growth rates of exports and imports in Korea became sluggish, and the openness ratio declined to approximately 85% in 2015. The sluggish growth rates of exports and imports in Korea during this period were attributed to the slow recovery of the world economy and also of the Korean economy. Furthermore, the worldwide resurgence of protectionist trade regimes exacerbated the situation. Given that the role played by export growth for Korea's economic growth has been quite substantial, the slow growth of Korea's exports will cast doubt over the future course of Korea's economic development.

Figure 2-1. Exports and Imports Growth Rates and the Openness in Korea, 1962-2015

Source: World Bank, World Development Indicators Database

• Transformation of Korea's Trade Structure

While the economic expansion for the last half century in Korea has accompanied the transformation of production structure, Korea's exports and import have also been structurally transformed. In the early 1960s, Korea's export was predominantly concentrated in the commodities and processed foods, accounting for approximately 75% of Korea's total export in 1962. From the early 1980s, however, the share of manufactures in Korea's total merchandise export increased rapidly, such that manufactured goods accounted for approximately 90% of the total exports (Figure 2-2).

Figure 2-2. Korea's Merchandise Exports, 1980-2015

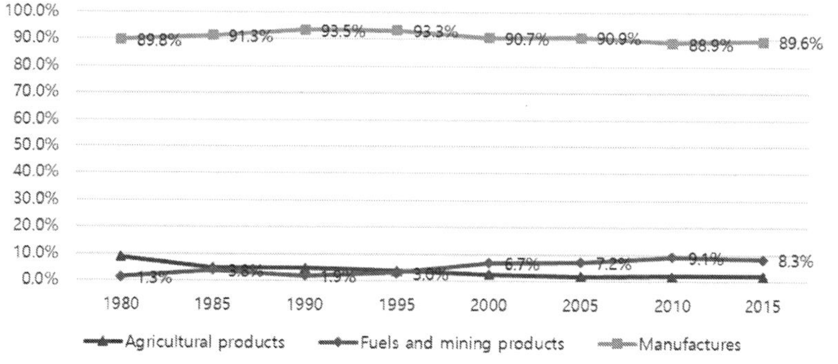

Source: WTO, Merchandise Trade Time Series Database

Even in the manufactures export, the structural changes have occurred. The four major export products in Korea such as iron and steel, chemicals, machinery and transportation equipment, and textiles, occupied approximately 52% of the total manufactures export in 1980. The share increased to 62.2% in 1990 and then to 80.7% in 2000. By 2015, the ratio further rose to 86.2%.

Since 1980, as seen in Figure 2-3, the export of machinery and transportation equipment took the largest share in the Korea's manufactures export. The ratio of this category increased from 22.7% in 1980 to 42.2% in 1990, and it further enlarged to 67.2% in 2005. The ratio slightly declined in the post-GFC period, and eventually it reached 66.0% in 2015. Over the same period, the proportion of chemicals in the total manufactures export has also revealed a similar trend. Thus, the ratio of this category amounted to 12.5% in 2015, having increased from

4.8% in 1980. Textiles has once been a star performing export product in Korea. However, its share continuously declined from 14.8% in 1980 to 4.8% in 2000 and further decreased to 2.3% by 2015.

Figure 2-3. Major Manufactures Exports in Korea, 1980-2015

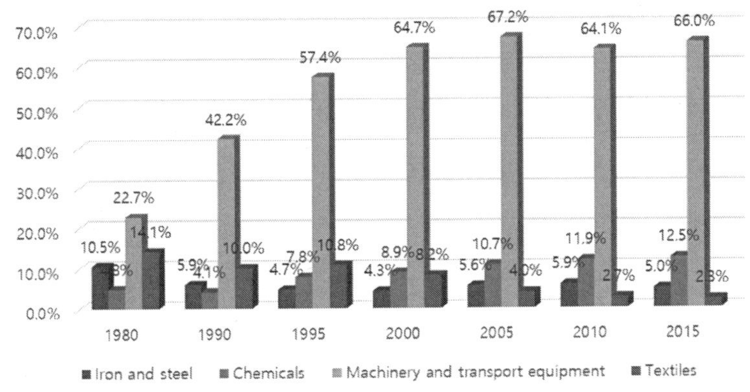

Source: WTO, Merchandise Trade Time Series Database

Figure 2-4. Korea's Merchandise Imports, 1980-2015

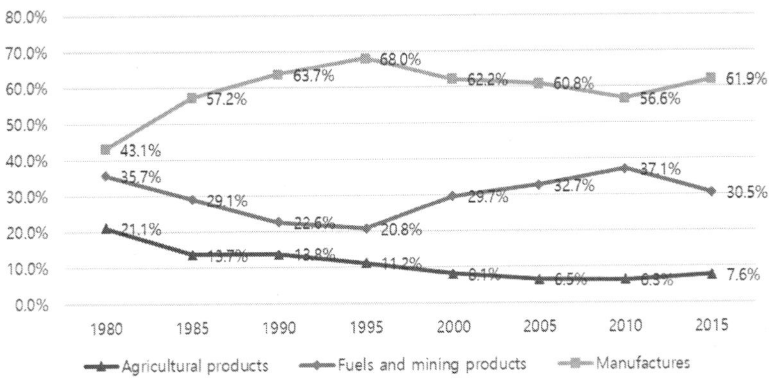

Source: WTO, Merchandise Trade Time Series Database

The rapid expansion of Korea's exports during the Korean economic development period has also accompanied a parallel increase of imports, reflecting Korea's poor natural resource endowment, food supply, as well as machineries and equipment supplies, as seen in Figure 2-4.

In the early-1960s, when Korea just implemented its first five-year economic development plan, Korea's import comprised mainly raw materials and equipment. Fertilizers, machineries, textiles, petroleum, steel products, and grains were among the top ten importables. Following the success of export promoting industrialization efforts, Korea's comparative advantage in labor intensive products began to erode rather quickly (Hong, 1980). From the early-1970s, thus, Korea switched over to creating dynamic comparative advantages by promoting heavily the heavy and chemical industries (HCI) (Jwa, 2001; Galbraith & Kim, 1998). However, the HCI drive, as it has commonly known in Korea, faced rampantly rising oil prices, twice in the 1970s. As a result, the import structure changed accordingly, such that petroleum and petroleum products remained Korea's most important import items, up until now, especially in the resource boom period of the 2000s. From 1980, nevertheless, manufactures import occupied the largest proportion of Korea's merchandise import.

Figure 2-5 shows Korea's bilateral trade with Iran during the period from 1970 to 2015. A few interesting observations can be made from the development of the bilateral trade between the two countries.

Firstly, trade volume increased rather rapidly during the period, from US$44 million in 1970 to US$6,098 million in 2015, equivalent to almost a 140-fold increase in nominal terms. Secondly, Korea had trade deficits with Iran almost throughout the period, except the early-1970s, i.e. 1972-1975, and 1981. Thirdly, Korea's exports to Iran steadily increased initially, and the increase accelerated since the early-2000s until recently when the international economic and financial sanctions on Iran came to its full effect, i.e. 2012 - 2014. Lastly, but not the least, the increases of Korea's imports from Iran coincided with the increase of international oil prices, notably from the early- to mid-1980s subsequent to the second oil price shocks, and from 2002 until the recent period when the recovery of the global economy from the global financial crisis staggered (Figure 2-6). The rapid increase of international oil prices from 2002 demonstrated a high correlation with Korea's import from Iran during the period and the overall trade. Thus, Korea's trade deficit with Iran consequently was exacerbated.

Figure 2-5. Korea's Trade with Iran, 1970-2015

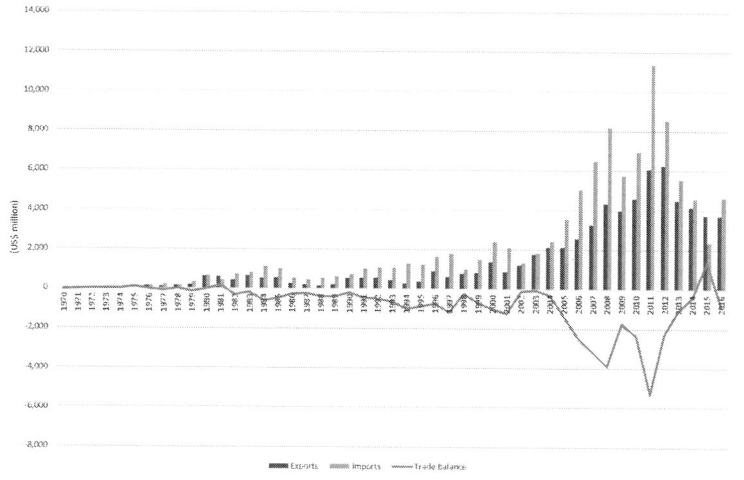

Source: kita.net

Figure 2-6. Crude Oil Price Movements, 1970 - 2016

Source: www.tradingeconomics.com

The particular observations made in the previous section, when combined with the natural resource endowment conditions of Korea and Iran, implied Korea and Iran might have mutually complementing economic and production structure. In fact, Korea's exports to Iran was predominantly manufactured goods, and whereas, Korea's imports from Iran was mainly natural resource related products in spite of the fact Iran has a relatively better developed manufacturing and industry sector, compared with other countries in the MENA region.

Figure 2-7. Structural Changes in Korea's Exports to Iran, 1990-2016

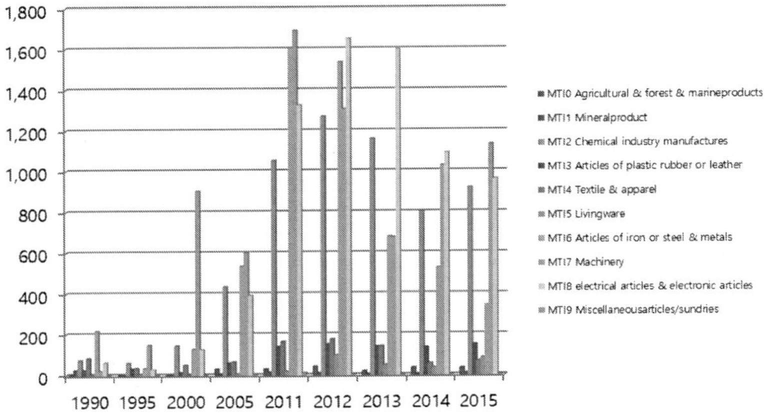

Source: kita.net

During the period 1990-2016, Korea's exports to Iran have experienced structural changes, as seen in Figure 2-7, even though Korea's export was predominantly manufactured products, ranging from MTI2 to MTI9.[32]

---

32 MTI codes used in this study represents the trade commodity classification used

In1990, Korea's largest export was MTI6, articles of iron or steel & metals, and it accounted for more than 46% of Korea's total export to Iran in that year (US$520 million). MTI4 (textile & apparel) occupied more than 16% of the share and was ranked at the second largest export category to Iran. MTI3 (articles of plastic rubber or leather) with 14.4% and MTI8 (electrical articles & electronic articles) with approximately 12.1% of the share followed in order.

Since 2000, four major categories dominated Korea's export to Iran whilst their respective shares fluctuated over time. They were MTI7 (machinery), MTI6 (articles of iron or steel & metals), MTI2 (chemical industry manufactures), and MTI8 (electrical articles & electronic articles). The combined share of these four categories hovered between approximately 91% and 93%, including the particular sanctions period 2012-2014, although rankings in terms of the importance as top exporting industries to Iran changed over time. In 2000, MTI7 (machinery) became the largest export industry with almost 65.7% of the share in Korea's total exports of US$1,375 million. From 2011, its share as the largest export category declined and reached to 15.1% in 2013. In the post-sanctions period 2015-2016, however, not only did its share recover, but it also attained the prime importance with 30.9% share

---

by Korea's Ministry of Trade and Industry and also by Korea's International Trade Association, which links with Korea's trade structure with Korea's industrial structure.

in 2016. MTI6 (articles of iron or steel & metals) reached the largest export share of 26.5% in 2011. After that year, its share decreased almost continuously and finally attained the share of 9.2% in Korea's US$3,717 million exports to Iran in 2016. MTI8 (electrical articles & electronic articles) continuously increased the share since 2005 until it achieved the largest export industry title with the share of 36.9% in 2014. But after that, the share decreased and reached 25.9% in 2016. The share of MTI2 (chemical industry manufactures) increased after 2005 and attained its largest share of 25.9% in Korea's total exports to Iran in 2013. However, after that year, the share has been slightly dropped and bounced back to 24.8% in 2016.

Unlike the structure of Korea's export to Iran, Korea's import structure has little changed during the 1990-2016, which can be seen in Figure 2-8. As expected, Korea's imports from Iran for this period has been predominantly MTI1 (mineral product), and its share has changed only marginally over the period between 95.9%, the lowest in 1995 and 2011, and 99.3%, the highest in 2014. While all other industry products' shares have been almost negligible or highly miniscule, MTI2 (chemical industry manufactures) has been the next important category on the Korea's import list from Iran which has once attained 3.3% share in 2011. From 2000, MTI6 (articles of iron or steel & metals) which had occupied approximately 2% in the 1990s has decreased its share to reach 0.4%, the lowest in 2014, during the sanctions period before its' share has rebounded back to 1.4% in 2016. The observations made above of the bilateral trade relations of Korea with Iran lend itself to assert that the trade structure between these two countries has been highly complementary and thus inter-industry trade.

Figure 2-8. The Structure of Korea's Imports from Iran, 1990 -2106

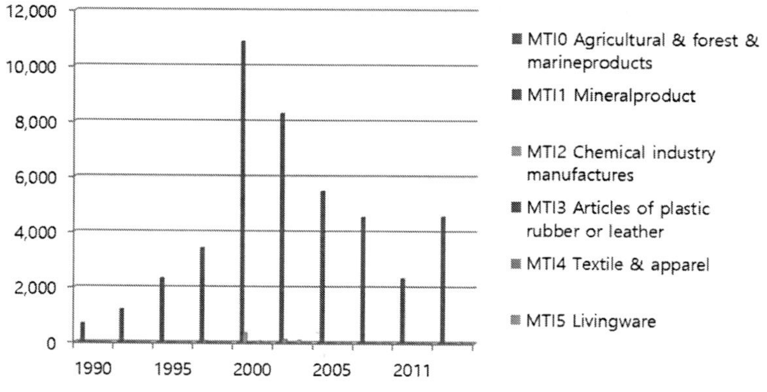

Source: kita.net

Complementing Trade Structure and Intra-Industry Trade between Korea and Iran —

In order to investigate the nature of trade further, more particularly whether or not the bilateral trade relation between Korea and Iran has approached intra-industry trade based on monopolistic competition and product differentiations, the Grubel-Lloyd intra-industry index (Grubel and Lloyd, 1975) has been adopted to measure the extent to which the bilateral trade is between the same or different industries during the period. Intra-industry trade means a simultaneous export and import of a good belonging to the same industry. The Grubel-Lloyd intra-industry trade index (GLIIT) of industry i is expressed as in its simplest form:

$$\text{IIT Index, } GLIIT_i = 1 - \frac{|X_i + M_i|}{(X_i + M_i)}, \quad 0 \leq GLIITi \leq 1$$

where X_i is the exports of industry i and M_i is industry i's imports. GLIIT =1 means the perfect intra-industry trade, and 0 means perfect inter-industry trade.

Although the Grubel-Lloyd intra-industry trade index possesses some caveats like aggregation bias because the level of industry classification influences the index value and its inadequacy with existence of multinational firms (see Egger et al., 2004, for example), the index is still the most popularly used in calculating the extent of trade within the same industry because of its intuitive appealing. In addition, in spite of the index at a certain industry level and the associate caveats, the dynamics of the index can show, at least, the extent of how much intra-industry trade changes over time, irrespective of the fact the limitations are still innate with.

For the period of 1990-2016, the bilateral trade data between Korea and Iran have been retrieved at the MTI 2-digit level. At the 2-digit level MTI, 56 industries were included in the calculations, but not all 56 industries were always included in the calculating the index values during the period due to either missing data or no trade data. The calculated GLIIT are provided in Table 2-3 for the selected years of 1990, 1995, 2000, 2005, 2010, 2015, and 2016.

Table 2-3. The Korea's Intra-Industry Trade Indices with Iran,1990-2016

Code	Nomenclature	1990	1995	2000	2005	2010	2015	2016
01	agricultural products/ farm produce	0.00	1.00	1.00	0.73	0.45	0.40	0.40
02	livestock rising					0.00	0.00	0.00
03	forest products	0.00						
04	fishery products					0.00	0.09	0.10
11	metal ore			0.00	0.00	0.00	0.00	0.00
12	base metal ore				0.00	0.00		0.00
13	mineral fuels	0.07	0.00	0.00	0.00	0.00	0.00	0.01
19	othermineral product							
21	petrochemicals	0.00	0.82	0.45	0.33	0.83	0.01	0.01
22	precision chemistry	0.00	0.22	0.10	0.29	0.84	0.00	0.00
23	fertilizers							
24	ceramic manufactures	1.00		0.00	0.00	0.00	0.00	0.00
25	materials of paper or articles of paper	0.00	0.00	0.00	0.00	0.00	0.00	0.00
26	articles of asbestos or mica							

27	articles of friction or grinding				0.00	0.00	0.00	0.00
29	other articles of chemical industry		0.00	0.00	0.00	0.00	0.00	0.00
31	articles of plastic rubber or leather	0.00	0.00	0.00	0.00	0.00	0.00	0.00
32	**articles of rubber**	**0.00**	**0.07**	**0.31**	**0.15**	**0.04**	**0.00**	**0.00**
33	articles of leather or fur			0.00		0.00		
41	materials of fiber	0.00	0.00	0.00	0.00	0.06	0.00	0.00
42	yarn	0.00	0.00	0.00	0.00	0.00	0.00	0.00
43	fabrics	0.00	0.00	0.00	0.00	0.00	0.00	0.00
44	**made-up textiles**	**0.00**	**0.00**	**1.00**	**0.00**	**0.00**	**0.00**	**0.00**
51	miscellaneous goods/ sundries					0.00	0.00	0.00
52	furniture					0.00	0.00	
53	musical instrument					0.00		
54	sport or hobby, recreation implements				0.00	0.00		
55	stationery	0.00	0.00		0.00	0.00		
56	toy							
57	art work	0.00	0.00	0.00				
59	other living ware				0.00	0.00		
61	**articles of iron or steel**	**0.00**	**0.80**	**0.05**	**0.05**	**0.01**	**0.00**	**0.00**
62	**nonferrous metal products**	**0.72**	**0.11**	**0.95**	**0.29**	**0.55**	**0.77**	**0.45**
63	table wares				0.00	0.00		
64	coin, nail and container							
69	other articles of steel metal			0.00	0.00	0.00	0.00	0.00
71	general machine	0.00	0.00	0.00	0.00	0.00	0.00	0.01
72	special machine	0.00	0.00	0.00	0.00	0.00	0.00	0.02

73	precision machine	0.00	0.00	0.00	0.00	0.00	0.00	0.00
74	transporter	0.00	0.00	0.00	0.00	0.00	0.00	0.00
75	mechanical elements, tools and metallic pattern	0.00	0.00	0.00	0.00	0.02	0.00	0.00
79	other machinery	0.00		0.00	0.00	0.00	0.00	0.00
81	industrial electronic articles	0.00	0.00	0.10	0.03	0.01	0.01	0.01
82	household electronic articles	0.00	0.00	0.00	0.00	0.00	0.00	0.00
83	electronic components	0.00	0.00	0.00	0.03	0.00	0.00	0.00
84	heavy electric equipment	0.00	0.00	0.00	0.00	0.00	0.00	0.00
85	electric wire	0.00		0.00	0.00	0.00		
91	printed matter							
92	works of art							
93	materials of collection							
94	spectacles and contact lens	0.00			0.00	0.00		
95	articles of medical care, hygiene				0.00	0.00	0.00	0.00
96	articles of gem, jewel and precious metal							
97	arms/weapon							
98	wig or false eyebrow							
99	other miscellaneous articles							

Source: Author's own calculation based on MTI 2-digit data retrieved from kita.net

This table deserves some interesting remarks. Firstly, only a handful of industries out of the total 56 industries have been allowed for the intra-industry index calculation during the period. Secondly, even those industries for which the GLIIT have been calculated and had the value greater than 0, the index value has been getting smaller over time, except MTI21 (petrochemicals) and MTI22 (precision chemistry).[33] MTI62 (non-ferrous metal products) is an interesting industry in that the GLIIT values have fluctuated widely during the period. Nevertheless, the GLIIT value in 2010 has shown 0.55 and increased to 0.77 in 2015 before it has decreased again to 0.45 in 2016. MTI01 (agricultural products / farm produce) is also interesting. Although the GLIIT value has decreased over time, it has still maintained the value persistently at 0.44 both in 2015 and 2016. Overall, the bilateral trade between Korea and Iran has predominantly taken place different industries, i.e. inter-industry trade, and thus it has affirmed that Korea's trade structure with Iran has been complementary.

33 Even in MTI21 (petrochemicals) and MTI22 (precision chemistry), the GLIIT for 2015 and 2016 are extremely low, but we attribute it to the early stage impact of lifting sanctions against Iran.

Korea's Outward FDI in Iran —

• Development of Korea's Outward FDI

For the period 1980-2016, Korea's outward foreign direct investment (OFDI, henceforth) has reached US$348.8 billion in terms of the cumulated investment amount for the 155,595 approved cases. As it can be seen in Figure 2-9, the major development of Korea's OFDI has been conducted mainly through three stages.

Figure 2-9. Korea's Outward Foreign Direct Investment

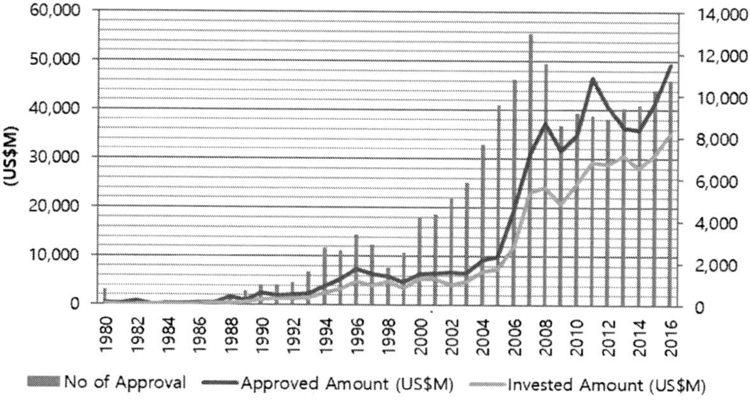

Source: Korea Export-Import Bank, Foreign Direct Investment Statistics database.

The first stage has begun from 1986 when OFDI has been liberalized following the political democratization and the subsequent industrial disputes which were combined with Korea's changing comparative advantage in manufacturing industries (Tcha, 1998). Around this time, the so-called push factors have contributed to rapidly rising OFDIs from Korea, and thus Korea's OFDI during this period has been dubbed as efficiency seeking FDI. The second stage of OFDI has occurred from the mid-1990s when Korea has joined the Organization for Economic Development and Cooperation (OECD) in 1995, and the Korean government has liberalized its capital account (Kim & Suh, 1998). During this time period, Korea's OFDI has been conducted not only in developing countries but also in developed countries. While those OFDI in developing countries has still remained as efficiency seeking, the latter OFDI made in developed countries have been called either market seeking or strategic asset seeking FDI (Moon, 2007). As the OFDI in developed countries originated from a developing country has been rare, Moon and Roehl (2001) have called this type of Korea's OFDI the imbalanced FDI.

Although the Asian financial crisis occurred during the second stage, it had not halted Korea's OFDI, but it has only slowed down the growing trend. In fact, Korea's OFDI during the period 1987-1997 has grown at the annual average growth rate of 35.8% (Ahn, 2008). In the post-Asian financial crisis period, however, Korea's OFDI has been recovered. Although the average growth rate of Korea's OFDI has slowed down to 7.9% over the period from 2000 to 2005, the amount of OFDI has reached US$23.1 billion for 12,973 approved cases in 2007 and US$24.2

billion for 11,576 approved cases in 2008 when the global financial crisis (GFC) has just hit the world economy. After a small set back in 2009, Korea's OFDI has quickly recovered in the post-GFC period, such that Korea's OFDI in 2016 has amounted to almost US$35.3 billion for 10,765 approved cases. Through the three stages of OFDI development in Korea, Seo (2017) has argued, Korean firms have been enabled to form global production networks, more conspicuously with countries in the East and South East Asian region.

Among the total cumulative OFDI from Korea during the period from 1980 to 2016, manufacturing has occupied the largest portion: it accounted for 48.8% of the total number of approved cases and 33.5% of the total invested amount (Table 2-4). The second largest sector has been mining. The mining industry had accounted for only 2.1% share in the total approved cases, but it occupied 16.8% of the total invested OFDI amount during the period. The importance of this particular sector has been almost self-explanatory, provided that Korea, as a natural resource deficient country, has placed one of highest priorities on securing energy supply and its security. Wholesale and retail trade has accounted for 15.4% of the total approved cases and 11.3% of the total invested OFDI amount in the same period. Finance and Insurance has occupied 1.7% of the number of approved cases and 11.1% of the total invested amount, and real estate and lease has explained 4.6% of the total approved cases and 9.6% of the total investment made. These two industries have ranked the third and fourth on the list of Korea's OFDI by industries.

Table 2-4. Korea's Outward Foreign Direct Investment, 1980-2016

	No. of Approval	No. of Establish ment	Approved Amount (US$M)	No of Transfers	Invested Amount (US$M)	No. of Approval	No. of Establish ment	Approved Amount	No of Transfers	Invested Amount
Total	171,167	69,580	497,982	270,624	352,909					
Agriculture, Forestry & Fishery	2,697	966	2,816	5,118	1,820	1.6%	1.4%	0.6%	1.9%	0.5%
Mining	3,586	772	99,915	13,557	59,211	2.1%	1.1%	20.1%	5.0%	16.8%
Manufacturing	83,561	32,115	151,739	144,095	118,253	48.8%	46.2%	30.5%	53.2%	33.5%
Electricity, Gas, Steam & Water	938	273	10,827	1,319	7,380	0.5%	0.4%	2.2%	0.5%	2.1%
Sewerage, Waste Management & Remediation Activities	258	101	122	346	99	0.2%	0.1%	0.0%	0.1%	0.0%
Construction	7,377	2,774	14,373	9,883	9,831	4.3%	4.0%	2.9%	3.7%	2.8%
Wholesale & Retail Trade	26,288	12,559	49,529	35,260	40,476	15.4%	18.0%	9.9%	13.0%	11.5%
Transportation and Storage	3,694	1,418	9,335	4,058	6,203	2.2%	2.0%	1.9%	1.5%	1.8%
Accommodation & Food Services	6,737	4,065	7,407	10,417	4,962	3.9%	5.8%	1.5%	3.8%	1.4%
Printing, Information & Communication	6,693	2,433	10,888	8,734	8,744	3.9%	3.5%	2.2%	3.2%	2.5%
Finance & Insurance	2,854	1,068	63,726	3,566	39,334	1.7%	1.5%	12.8%	1.3%	11.1%
Real Estate & Lease	7,942	3,121	49,703	11,417	33,738	4.6%	4.5%	10.0%	4.2%	9.6%
Professional, Scientific & Technical	6,114	2,458	21,116	7,966	18,682	3.6%	3.5%	4.2%	2.9%	5.3%

Administrative & Supportive Service	5,105	1,832	1,624	4,573	1,045	3.0%	2.6%	0.3%	1.7%	0.3%
Public Administration & Defense& Social Security	40	22	32	80	21	0.0%	0.0%	0.0%	0.0%	0.0%
Education	1,292	652	484	2,045	366	0.8%	0.9%	0.1%	0.8%	0.1%
Human Health & Social Work	611	251	432	1,027	309	0.4%	0.4%	0.1%	0.4%	0.1%
Art, Entertainment & Recreation	1,985	762	2,900	3,359	1,809	1.2%	1.1%	0.6%	1.2%	0.5%
Other Services	2,562	1,733	942	3,500	593	1.5%	2.5%	0.2%	1.3%	0.2%
Activities of households as Employers	16	6	8	14	1	0.0%	0.0%	0.0%	0.0%	0.0%
Activities of Extraterritorial Organizations and Bodies	1	1	0	1	0	0.0%	0.0%	0.0%	0.0%	0.0%
N/A	816	198	64	289	31	0.5%	0.3%	0.0%	0.1%	0.0%

Source: Korea Export-Import Bank, Foreign Direct Investment Statistics database.

Table 2-5. Korea's Outward Foreign Direct Investment Made, 2009-2016

	No. of Approval	No. of Establishment	Approved Amount	No. of Transfers	Invested Amount
Total (out of the total 1980-2016)	44.3%	34.5%	63.6%	43.5%	64.8%
Agriculture, Forestry & Fishery	41.5%	22.0%	48.6%	40.8%	55.8%
Mining	55.2%	40.5%	74.9%	54.8%	80.4%
Manufacturing	38.3%	27.3%	51.0%	37.0%	54.2%
Electricity, Gas, Steam & Water	85.3%	79.1%	87.1%	85.1%	90.1%

Sewerage, Waste Management & Remediation Activities	67.1%	60.4%	78.6%	69.4%	82.3%
Construction	57.9%	48.4%	57.7%	56.9%	66.1%
Wholesale & Retail Trade	**48.5%**	**41.9%**	**49.7%**	**49.9%**	**48.5%**
Transportation and Storage	52.4%	47.7%	74.5%	59.9%	72.1%
Accommodation & Food Services	38.0%	31.1%	50.0%	37.8%	53.2%
Printing, Information & Communication	62.0%	56.5%	55.2%	62.0%	58.5%
Finance & Insurance	**70.6%**	**59.8%**	**82.3%**	**75.0%**	**78.9%**
Real Estate & Lease	**34.3%**	**28.0%**	**72.2%**	**36.7%**	**78.2%**
Professional, Scientific & Technical	66.8%	54.0%	61.1%	66.1%	63.9%
Administrative & Supportive Service	46.0%	36.2%	51.8%	55.0%	46.9%
Public Administration & Defense & Social Security	60.0%	36.4%	48.8%	77.5%	25.0%
Education	50.2%	45.2%	41.0%	47.7%	44.9%
Human Health & Social Work	54.8%	32.3%	58.2%	52.7%	59.8%
Art, Entertainment & Recreation	41.0%	23.9%	34.8%	37.2%	33.0%
Other Services	27.4%	22.7%	20.5%	23.9%	19.8%
Activities of households as Employers	12.5%	33.3%	0.2%	14.3%	1.4%
Activities of Extraterritorial Organizations and Bodies	100.0%	100.0%	100.0%	100.0%	100.0%
N/A	40.8%	24.2%	61.1%	47.8%	23.7%

Source: Korea Export-Import Bank, Foreign Direct Investment Statistics database

One interesting observation regarding the Korea's OFDI is that the OFDI in the mining industry which has ranked as the second largest sector for Korea's OFDI during the period 1980-2016 has been conducted mainly in the-post GFC period. In fact, out of the total invested amount of US$59.2 billion in the mining industry, more than 80% has been made over the period from 2009 to 2016. Whereas, in the manufacturing industry that has taken the lion's share in the same period in terms of the number of the approved cases, approximately 54% of the total invested amount has been conducted also in the post-GFC period (Table 2-5).

- **Iran, an Outlier of Korea's OFDI**

During 1980-2016, Korea's direct investment in Iran has been miniscule and erratic in the sense that the total invested OFDI in Iran from Korea has amounted only to US$54 million[34] for 74 approved cases, as seen in Figure 2-10. Interestingly, the majority of Korea's OFDI has taken place during the crisis periods, i.e. 1997 - 1998 and 2008 – 2009. The total invested amount conducted during these two periods has amounted to US$43million, accounting for more than 79% of

34 The approved amount was US$ 109 million during this period.

the total invested amount in Iran by Korean firms between 1980 and 2016. In terms of the industry distribution for Korea's OFDI in Iran, manufacturing sector has absorbed US$47 million of the investment for 34 approved cases, accounting for approximately 87% of the total invested amount and 46% of the number of approvals during the 1980-2016 (Table 2-6).

Figure 2-10. Korea's Direct Investment in Iran, 1980-2016

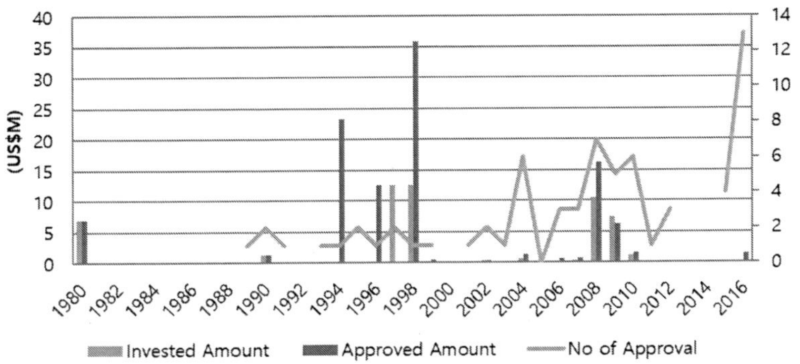

Source: Korea Export-Import Bank, Foreign Direct Investment Statistics database

Table 2-6. Korea's OFDI in Iran by Sector, 1980-2016

	No. of Approval	No. of Establishment	Approved Amount (US$M)	No. of Transfers	Invested Amount (US$M)
Total	74	28	109	52	54
Mining	1	1	0	1	0
Manufacturing	34	17	101	40	47
Construction	10	5	7	5	7

Wholesale and Retail Trade	11	1	0	2	0
Transportation & Storage	1	0	0	0	0
Printing, Information & Communication	1	0	0	0	0
Finance & Insurance	2	0	1	0	0
Professional, Scientific & Technical	2	1	0	1	0
Administrative & Supportive Service	6	3	0	3	0
N/A	6	0	0	0	0

Source: Korea Export-Import Bank, Foreign Direct Investment Statistics database.

As for the development of Korea's OFDI, Iran has been left out as an outlier even though it has been supplying a significant amount of crude oil to Korea. However, Korea's OFDI during this period is in quite a stark contrast with what Iran has attracted OFDI from the world although the actual information on FDI in Iran has been quite sketchy.

As seen in Figure 2-11, FDI inflows to Iran has been erratic during the post-1979 Revolution period, including numerous divestments in the 1980s, as well as the rapidly increased FDI flows to Iran in the early 2000s, which has coincided with the global resource boom period.

In 2007 the industrial sector, including food and beverage, tobacco, textiles, clothing, leather, chemical, steel, and oil derivates had received the largest amount of FDI inflows to Iran, and the amount has exceeded US$8.76 billion. Water, electricity, and gas sector has ranked the second by attracting US$874.83 million. In the third place, the real estate sector has ranked by absorbing more than US$406 million. Investments in service, telecommunication, transportation, and mines reached $193 million, $14.3 million and $14.2 million, respectively (Miraskari et al. 2014, p. 230). In 2012 when international sanctions on Iran has been intensified, however, FDI inflows to Iran has declined substantially until it has slowly been able to resume in 2015 with the agreement on nuclear development program abandonment and lift the sanctions against Iran. In its first year of the post-sanction lift period, Iran has attracted US$11.8 billion FDI, which was six times higher than the amount in 2015. An optimistic forecast has been made on that Iran would be able to attract US$15 billion by the end of the 2016 Iranian fiscal year (Zhanalty, 2017).

Figure 2-11, FDI Inflows to Iran from the World and Korea, 1980-2016

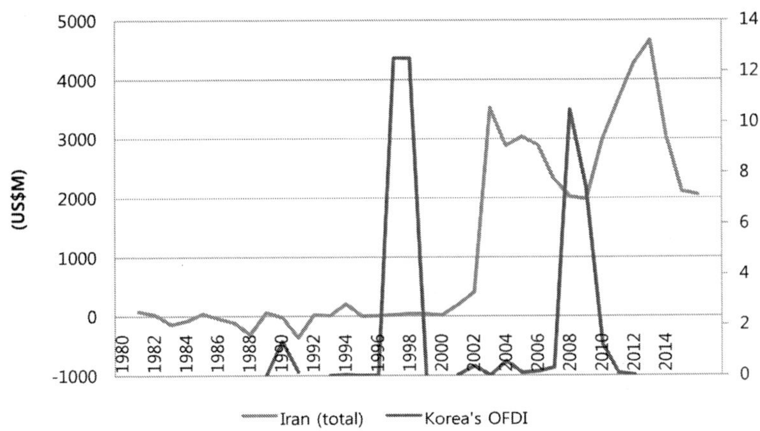

Source: Korea Export-Import Bank, Foreign Direct Investment Statistics database, and UNCTAD.

In terms of the sectoral distribution of the approved FDI flows to Iran, water and energy sector (including renewables) has received the largest amount with US$8.1 billion for 35 projects. Services and tourism sector have managed to attract FDI to 17 projects worth $1.53 billion, ranking the second position. Industry and mining sector has received $1.53 billion for 48 projects. In addition, agricultural sector had attracted US$512 million for 8 projects, and transportation and telecommunication sector has recieved US$259 million for 3 projects (Zhanalty, 2017).

CONCLUSION —

Korea has experienced a remarkable economic growth since the early-1960s through even more rapidly expanding external trade, particularly exports. During the course of Korea's economic development, Korea's export sector has formed its international production networks through the stages of OFDI development, especially with countries in the East and South East Asian regions (Seo, 2017). The import sector in Korea has also expanded, paralleling the rapidly expanding export sector, reflecting Korea's resource endowment conditions as well as for the import of parts and intermediate products.

Thus, resource rich countries like Iran have been faithful suppliers of energy sources and minerals, and Korea's trade balance with Iran has been chronically in deficit almost entirely throughout the period from 1970 to 2016. The trade deficit seemed to have widened during the international resource boom in the 2000s.

The formation of international production networks has been further facilitated by the OFDI conducted by Korean firms and businesses, especially in the manufacturing sector which has accounted for more than 33.5% of the Korea's total invested OFDI during the period 1980-2016. The conspicuously notable observation of this period was the globalization of Korean firms and businesses through OFDI which has been further accelerated in the post-GFC period. In this particular period, however, the security of a stable resource supply has become of prime importance. So, Korea's OFDI during the period has focused on the mining sector to the extent that the second largest amount of OFDI from Korea has been made in this sector. The total invested OFDI in mining has amounted to US$59.2 billion, and more than 80% of it has been conducted in the post-GFC period. Despite this remarkable upsurge of OFDI in mining, and to certain extent in manufacturing, Iran has failed to attract Korea's OFDI, no matter how we pay our attention to, the entire period from 1980 to 2016 or more specifically to a shorter period of the post-GFC era 2009-2016.

Currently, the sixth five-year development plan is undergoing in Iran (2016 – 2020), during which the Iranian economy is projected to grow at annual rate of 8%. That projection in the post-sanctions lift period in Iran sounds not unreasonable since Iran is allowed to access to the global oil and commodities markets. One of the priority policy agenda facing Iran is to attract as much FDI as possible in order to best recoup the benefits that are expected to accrue during the post-sanctions lift era. Even in Iran, FDI is considered the prime modality for stimulating economic and industrial development because it is regarded as a package of capital, technology, management know-hows, and markets.

With the sanctions lifted in Iran, the sectors which are expected to receive FDI inflows are oil and energy sector, automobile, and pharmaceuticals. According to the Iranian official forecast, oil and gas sector alone will need US$130-150 billion new investments by 2020 in order to prevent oil production from falling (The World Bank, 2015). Thus, Korean firms and businesses need to be ready to capitalize that opportunities provided by the Iranian economic prospects through understanding better cultural, legal, religious aspects, and economic idiosyncrasies that Iran bears. That kind of efforts and subsequent cooperation between the two countries may contribute to the revival of the maritime Silk Road.

References

Ahn, C.Y. (2008). *New direction of Korea's foreign direct investment policy in the multi-track FTA era: Inducement and aftercare services*, OECD Global Forum on International Investment.

Choi, N.S. (2016). An analysis of economic effects of the Korea-Iran economic cooperation and implications for Korean businesses. *KERI Policy Research*, 2016-11. Korea Economic Research Institute. (Korean)

Egger, H., Egger, P., & Greenaway, D. (2004). Intra-industry trade with multinational firms: theory, measurement and determinants. *Research Paper Series*, 2004/10. Leverhulme Center for Research on Globalization and Economic Policy, University of Nottingham.

Galbraith, J.K., & Kim, J. (1998). The legacy of the HCI: An empirical analysis of Korean Industrial Policy. *Journal of Economic Development*, 23(1), 1-20.

Grubel, H., & Lloyd, P. (1975). *Intra-Industry trade: The theory and measurement of international trade in differentiated products.* London: MacMillan.

Heo, Y. (2001). Development strategy in Korea reexamined: An interventionist perspective. *The Social Science Journal*, 38, 217-231.

Hong, W.T. (1987). Export-oriented growth and trade patterns in Korea.

In C. Braford, Jr. & W.H. Branson (Eds.). *Trade and structural change in Pacific Asia* (pp. 273-306). University of Chicago Press.

Jwa, S.H. (2001). *A new paradigm for Korea's economic development: From government control to market economy.* New York, N.Y.: Palgrave.

Kim, D.C., & Suh, D.S. (1998). Financial liberalization and Korean corporations' financing policy for globalization. *Journal of Asian Economics*, 9(1), 31-66.

Kim, K.S. (1991). The Korean miracle (1962-1980) revisited: Myths and realities in strategy and development. *Working Paper #* 166, November. Kellogg Institute.

Lee, H.S. (2011). The survey of new discovery, analysis and interpretation of ancient manuscripts and literary materials on Korean studies in the Middle East. *KIEP Research Material*, 11-51.

Miraskari, S. R., Masouleh, M. S., & Alavi, S.A. (2014). Analyzing impacts of foreign direct investment on private sector in economic growth of Iran. *International Journal of Academic Research in Business and Social Sciences*, 4(11), 223-237.

Moon, H.C., & Roehl T.W. (2001). Unconventional foreign direct investment and the imbalance theory. *International Business Review*, 10(2), 197-215.

Moon, H.C. (2007). Outward foreign direct investment by enterprises from the Republic of Korea. In *Global players from emerging markets: Strengthen enterprise competitiveness through outward investment* (pp. 93-106). New York and Geneva: United Nations

Seo, J.S. (2017), Free trade agreement as a facilitator for cross border trade and foreign direct investment in Korea: implications for the Korea-Australia cooperation. A paper presented at *the 2017 Korea-Australia Next Generation Policy Experts Forum*, April 27-28, Canberra, Australia.

Seo, J.S., & Suh, C.S. (2006). An analysis of home country trade effects of outward foreign direct investment: The Korean experience with ASEAN, 1987-2002. *ASEAN Economic Bulletin*, 23(2), 160-170.

Tcha, M.J. (1998). Labor disputes and direct foreign investment: The experience of Korea in transition. *Economic Development and Cultural Change*, 46(2), 305-327.

The World Bank. (2015). Economic implications of lifting sanctions on Iran. *Mena Quarterly Economic Brief*, Issue 5, July.

The World Factbook. (2017). CIA. https://www.cia.gov/library/publications/resources/the-world-factbook/index.html.

Valadkhani, A. (2001). An analysis of Iran's third five-year development plan in the post-Revolution era (2000-2005). *Research Online*. University of Wollongong.

Yoo, I. (2008). Korea's economic development: Lessons and suggestions for developing countries. *Korean Social Science Journal*, 35(1), 31-63.

Zhanaltay, Zhengizkhan (2017). Foreign direct investment flows to Iran in the post-sanctions period. *Weekly e-Bulletin*, 102. Eurasian Research Institute.

Iran in the Changing World: Outsiders' Perspective

III

Islamic Banking in Iran

Yoonmin Kim, Keimyung University

III

Islamic Banking in Iran

Yoonmin Kim

Abstract —

Islamic banking, an alternate to interest-based banking is not banking in the traditional sense. It derives its inspiration and guidance from the religious edicts of Islam, and its operations are strictly in accordance with the directives of Islamic law. Islamic financial system employed the concept of participation in the enterprise, utilizing the funds at risk on the profit-and-loss-sharing basis. Islamic banks have developed profit sharing schemes in tapping and mobilizing their resources. In relation to entrepreneurs, the status of an Islamic bank is either of partner or investor, whereas for the conventional banks the relationship is more of creditor-debtor.

This study traced out the growth of Islamic banking in Iran in which banking activities have been completely transformed to comply with the accepted Islamic principles. The banking system of Iran is being perceived as an effective tool in pursuing Islamic economic objectives. However, Islamic banking in Iran is currently facing tough times in the wake of dire economic sanctions imposed against them, and thus it needs to introduce effective corporate governance and a better interaction with relevant international, regional, and national institutions, so that it can continue the perceived contributions for the welfare of people and community as a whole.

Keywords
Islamic Banking, usury-Riba, Islamization, interest free, Gharz-al-hasaneh, Mozaraah, Mosharekat, Mozarebeh, Joaalah, and Mosaqat

Islamic Banking Theories and Basis —

Islamic banks are banks that follow Sharia (Islamic law) in their business transactions. Among other things, Sharia prohibits dealing in loans that charge interest, undertaking transactions with unknown fate (Gharar), requiring transactions to be lawful (halal), and that Muslims pay a religious tax (Zakah). Abolishing interest from their dealings is the fundamental principle on which Islamic banks are based. Islam's strict ban on dealing with interest seems to have social roots. Use of Riba (usury) violates the principle of social justice, which is very important in Islam, because it leads to rewarding people without them making an effort. Those that charge interest when lending money do not participate in the risks of the projects financed or make any effort in a borrower's endeavor other than lending, and such behaviors are rejected in the teachings of Islam. Interest-based transactions allow lenders to receive the advantages associated with lending money, while avoiding the risks and losses that a borrower may experience. The most apparent reason for banning Riba is to enforce the spirit of brotherhood between Muslims. The major prohibited elements under Sharia are Riba (interest), Gharar (uncertainty), Maisir (gambling), Haram (prohibited) food and drinks, and immoral activities.

From the viewpoint of Islamic Sharia, the banking system has to avoid interest in order to be justified within Islam. Consequently, financial intermediation in Islamic banking between the bank and the client takes place as a partnership rather than a debtor-creditor relationship. The financial activities of modern conventional banks are based on the creditor-debtor relationship between depositors and banks on the one hand and between borrowers and banks on the other. Interest is regarded by conventional banks as the price of extending credit and reflects the opportunity cost of money. Because Islam prohibits interest, however, commercial banking in the Islamic framework cannot be based on the creditor-debtor relationship.

Another aspect of the theoretical bases of Islamic banking is the interest free bank does not mean risk free. This principle is applicable to two main production factors, i.e. labor and capital. According to this principle, since no payment is allowed toward labor upon lending unless it is applied to work, no reward for lending capital should be allowed unless there is an exposure to business risks.

Islamic Banking Promotes a Responsible Free Market Economy —

Islam somehow defines certain limits on economic activities. A Muslim believes that Islam do not restrict economic activities but instead direct it toward responsible activities that benefit other people, protect the earth, or honor Allah. In other words, Islam allows for a free market economy where supply and demand are decided in the market, not dictated by a government. But at the same time, Islam directs the function of the market mechanism by imposing specific laws and ethics.

One important purpose of imposing laws and ethics is to promote social justice. Islam and social justice are inseparable, and as such it is a key concept of the Islamic financial industry. Social justice in Islamic finance means "Believing that Allah is the owner of wealth." Islam does not allow for a society where a small number of people enjoy most of the wealth, while many people have very little. Economically speaking, social justice is the distribution of wealth in the way that helps correct such an imbalance.

Islam tries to achieve social justice in the economy in the following ways:

① Promoting adherence to Islam: A Muslim is expected to adhere to certain core beliefs and perform certain obligatory acts. By reminding Muslims of their obligations, Islam seeks to promote stronger relationships between each person and Allah, between people and the earth, and among individuals. Islam affirms that when humans believe in Allah and follow his commandments, they create harmony on earth by behaving responsibly. Striving for social justice is the key to this harmony.

② Requiring Zakat: By taxing the property of people who acquire wealth and distributing that tax to people in need, Islam promotes the socially responsible distribution of wealth.

③ Defining the state's obligations: Per Islam, the state (meaning a nation's or city's leaders or government) is also responsible for ensuring that social justice exists. Islamic scholars argue the state should collect zakat and guide wealth distribution to make sure that everyone's basic needs are provided for. In addition, scholars generally agree that states should protect the real value of money by implementing sound fiscal policy.

④ Prohibiting usury (interest): Islam prohibits interest-based transactions. It does so for the sake of social justice. No individual or business entity should hoard money in order to earn interest; instead, people and businesses should use money to support productive economic activities that create investment, trading, and jobs. The returns of successful economic activities are then distributed to the different parties involved. In other words, wealth should be shared.

⑤ Encouraging shared risk: Islam also promotes social justice by encouraging risk-sharing in economic transactions. When risk is shared among two or more parties involved in an economic activity, the burden of the risk faced by each party is reduced.

Brief History of Banking in Iran —

Iran has instituted an Islamic banking system, while many other Islamic countries have established "mixed" systems that combine aspects of Western and Islamic banking practices. Iran began its interest-free banking system in 1979 when it nationalized its commercial banks. The process was accelerated in 1980 when the Money and Credit Council of the Central Bank of the Islamic Republic of Iran reduced the interest rate charged by commercial banks against borrowers and that paid to depositors. In April 1983, the Iranian government submitted the Islamic banking bills to the Iranian unicameral legislative body. Once approved by the legislative body and subsequently by the Council of Guardians (a body that sanctions the compatibility of all laws with the Islamic tenets), the Islamic banking bill became law on March 21, 1984. This law banned the payment of interest on all lending and borrowing activities. The central tenet of an economic system based on Islamic principles is the absolute prohibition on the payment and receipt of interest. Fundamentally, it is this prohibition that makes Islamic banks and financial institutions in Iran different from their Western counterparts.

• **Gharz-al-hasaneh**

Gharz-al-hasaneh is a term for an interest-free loan given by an Islamic bank to needy people in the society. In other words, it is an interest-free loan extended by the bank to a real or legal person for a definite period of time. The practice of dealing with this sort of investment differs from bank to bank. Gharz-al-hasaneh is normally given to needy students, small producers, farmers, entrepreneurs, and economically weaker sections of the society, who are not in a position to obtain a loan or any financial assistance from any other institutional sources. The main aim of this loan is to help needy people in the society in order to make them self-sufficient and raise their income and the standard of living.

In other words, Gharz-al-hasaneh means beneficence loans. These are zero-return loans that the Koran exhorts Muslims to make available to those who need them. Financial organizations that provide these loans are permitted to charge the borrower a service fee to cover administrative costs of handling the loan so long as the fee is not related to the amount or the time period of the loan and solely represents the cost of administrating the loan.

• **Mozaraah (sharing profit and loss with venture capital)**

Mozaraah is a contract based on a financial partnership where one party (an investor) gives money to another (a fund manager) for the purpose of investing it in a business or economic activity. The investor puts up all the capital, and the fund manager provides expertise and knowledge to help the activity be successful. Both parties share the profits based on an agreed-upon ratio, but only the investor can lose the initial capital if the activity is not successful.

In a Mozaraah equity financial contract, an investor engages with an entrepreneur who has expertise in a particular field. The result is a partnership contract where both parties share the profits and losses. The profit and loss sharing (PLS) ratio is decided in advance by both parties based on what each of them brings to the table.

A Mozaraah contract is based on the partnership where one partner is the financier (investor or silent partner), and the other partner (the fund manager or working partner) manages the financier's investment in an economic activity. The second partner (often an entrepreneur) has expertise in applying the venture capital to the economic activities. Both parties agree in advance to a PLS ratio.

In this contract, the basic factors of production from the Islamic economics view point are capital, labor, and entrepreneurship, which are combined to make an economic activity. The investor provides the capital, and the fund manager gets a portion of the profit for his effort, and the investor gets the remaining profits. All Mozaraah contracts are limited by a specific time period, and they do not continue indefinitely.

Mozaraah contracts can also serve as a source of funds for an Islamic bank. When customers deposit money and expect a return, they are investors. The bank is the fund manager or work partner. The bank invests the depositor's money according to sharia guidelines.

Investors can choose to invest in two types of Mozaraah contracts.

Restricted Mozaraah: The investor specifies a particular business or project for which the investment funds are to be used. The working partner should not use the funds for any other business or project.

Unrestricted Mozaraah: In this Mozaraah contract, the investor gives the working partner a permission to funnel the funds into any type of business or project that best suits the financial goals of both partners.

When a Mozaraah contract is used as the source of bank funds (when the customer deposits money in the bank), the unrestricted Mozaraah is most often used. When the contract supports a bank's equity financial product (when the bank supplies funds to a working partner), the restricted Mozaraah is most often in play.

With Mozaraah contracts, the investor and the fund manager share profits and losses based on an agreed-upon ratio. The manager or working partner also receives a fixed fee for managing the project, in addition to the share of any profits.

If the economic venture results in a loss, that loss is absorbed sorely by the investor as the capital provider unless the fund manager has acted negligently or has engaged in misconduct. In other words, if the fund manager does not act in good faith, he is on the hook for the financial losses incurred.

Figure 3-1. The MozaraahContract in Action as a Financial Instrument

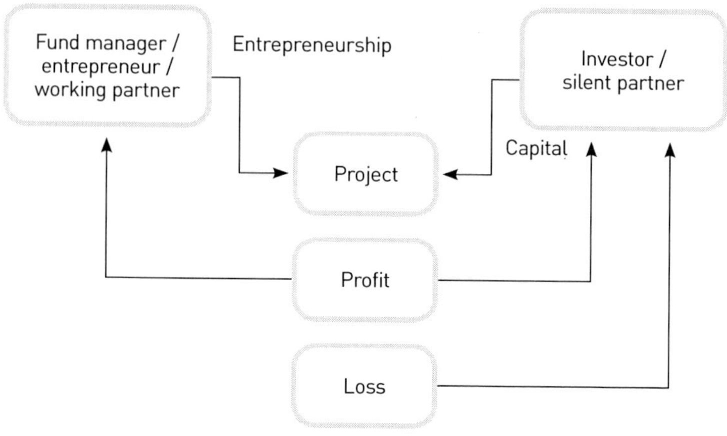

 The Mozaraah contract is applied when someone deposits money in an Islamic bank with an expectation of getting returns. In most cases, the contract applied is a first-tier (simple) Mozaraah contract, meaning that only the customer and the bank are involved. The bank serves as a fund manager for whatever money is deposited.

However, another type of contract exists which is a two-tier (intermediary) Mozaraah contract. In this case, the bank acts as an intermediary between the depositor and the bank's clients to whom it provides money. In other words, the Islamic bank acts as an intermediary between the investor and the entrepreneur. Islamic scholars promote using this kind of Mozaraah model in two scenarios:

① The bank on its own does not have the capacity to serve as the investor. This scenario may mean that the bank does not have enough liquidity to enter a Mozaraah contract with an entrepreneur or fund manager.

② The bank lacks the expertise to serve as the fund manager for an investment. In both cases, the two-tier contract allows the bank to create a link between investors and an expert fund manager or entrepreneur, so the economic activity can take place.

Figure 3-2. The two-tier Mozaraah Contract

The two-tier method of Mozaraah is less-frequently applied than the first-tier method. That is because banks usually have the liquidity and/or expertise to enter into a first tier contract and because the two-tier method is not quite as profitable for the bank as the first-tier method.

• Mosharekat (supporting joint venture)

Mosharekat is a joint venture contract. All parties invest capital up front, and all share profit and loss based on an agreed-upon ratio. One party (a bank) may be a nonworking investor, meaning that another party (the working partner) would be compensated in the profit ratio for the time and expertise contributed to the venture.

Mosharekat contracts allow both the bank and the customer to contribute to a project in the form of technical assistance, capital, working capital, or expertise. Both parties share the profits and losses, according to the contract terms. In this joint venture, all parties may contribute some (not necessarily an equal) percentage of all three factors of economic production (capital, labor, and entrepreneurship).

In a Mozaraah contract, one party is a financier (silent partner), and the other party (working partner) provides labor and entrepreneurship. But in the Mosharekat contract, all participants are working partners. Islamic banks use the Mosharekat contract to finance trade, provide working capital, and support other large projects. Based on the Mosharekat contract, the Islamic bank provides letters of credit to its customers who deal in international trade. The Mosharekat contract is a limited partnership that supports customers who lack sufficient funds to import what they need. A customer supplies part of the money, the bank supplies the rest, and the bank issues the letters of credit. Then, after the imported items arrive, one of three scenarios applies:

① Islamic bank sells its share in the Mosharekat to the customer on cash payment or a deferred basis at an agreed margin.

② The customer sells its share to the Islamic bank via cash payment or a deferred basis

③ Both sell their shares in the market together

Figure 3-3. The Mosharekat Contract

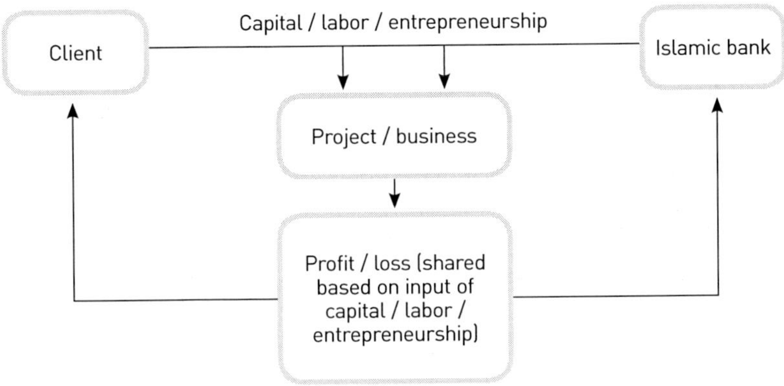

Islamic banks divide Mosharekat products into two categories based on the retention of the partners in the joint venture, i.e. how long the partners will stay in the joint venture.

① Consecutive partnership (consecutive Mosharekat): Each partner can keep its share in the partnership until the very end of the joint venture, project, or business. However, the partners are often allowed to withdraw or transfer their shares (unless the initial contract especially states that all the partners shall remain in the partnership until the date of maturity). If one of the partners withdraws from the contract, however, the whole partnership does not terminate.

② Declining balance partnership (diminishing Mosharekat): One partner is allowed to buy the other partner's share of equity step by step until the whole equity of the other partner is transferred. It is called a declining balance partnership because one partner's equity balance declines gradually.

• Mozarebeh (managing trade financing)

Mozarebeh is a "cost plus" contract used to finance working capital and assets and secure letters of credit. Both parties in contact agree to a sales price that includes profits for the seller and the financer. The profits must be clearly indicated when the agreement is formed. Until the money is paid back (in a one-time payment or over time in deferred installments), the bank owns whatever item is being financed.

In the Mozarebeh partnership contract, one party gives money to another party that invests in a business or economic activity. Both parties share any profits made from the investment (based on a pre-agreed ratio), but only the investor (the first party) can lose money if the investment goes wrong.

In this kind of agreement, a commodity is sold for cost plus profits, and both the buyer and the seller know the cost and the profits involved. Basically, this product is a kind of trade financing instrument used by Islamic banks.

Under the Mozarebeh contract, a bank purchases a commodity in order to supply it to the customer who is not financially able to make such a purchase directly. The bank sells the commodity to the customer for the cost plus profits (the profits being a markup that both the bank and the customer agree on upfront). The customer can make a lump sum payment when the commodity is delivered; however, a deferred payment installment schedule is usually set up.

Sharia scholars do not advocate using the deferred payment system in the Mozarebeh contract. Instead, they encourage using Mozarebeh as a financial instrument only when other equity financing does not suit the type of arrangement being entered into. The bank is allowed to take assets as security against potential future default by the client. However, when no such assets are available, the bank can take the commodity that is financed by the bank.

The Mozarebeh contract is a basic sales transaction, and certain rules need to be followed to make sure it does not foster sharia-complaints.

③ If the client defaults on the payment, the financier is not allowed to charge extra fees such as a late payment fee or penalty charges. Sharia scholars allow charging additional fees in thc casc of loss or damage due to the client's default, and they allow certain penalties in order to ensure that a buyer is not negligent. But such fees and penalties cannot be treated as income for the bank. They must be given to charity.

④ The contract should be used only for purchases. It is now intended to be used for financing a working capital requirement.

Figure 3-4. The Mozarebeh Contract in Action

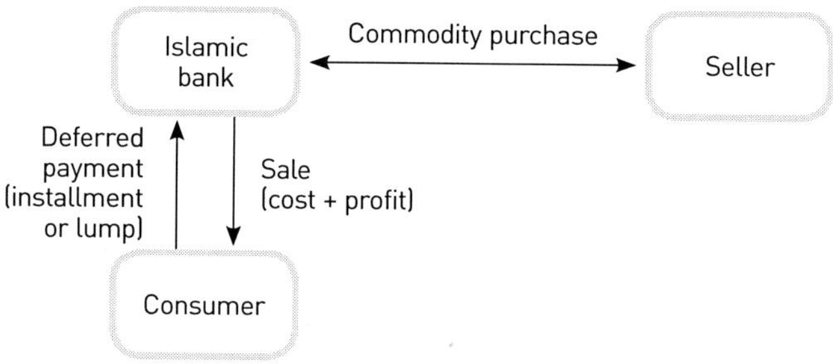

Here are two types of Mozarebeh contracts an Islamic bank may offer:

① Mozarebeh to the purchase orderer: In this contract, the bank specially purchases the assets for the client's order. The client requests that the bank purchase the goods on her behalf, and she agrees to buy the goods from the banks.

② Commodity Mozarebeh: Interbank transactions are a source

of funds for Islamic banks. The commodity of Mozarebeh is used as an instrument in Islamic interbank transactions. Generally, this financial instrument is used to fund the Islamic bank's short-term liquidity requirements; this product was developed as an alternative to the conventional interbank funding. Commodities such as gold, silver, barley, salt, wheat, and dates that are used as mediums of exchange, are not allowed to be traded under the commodity Mozarebeh contract.

- **Joaalah (financing construction projects)**

Joaalah is a deferred delivery contract that comes into play in financing construction projects. The buyer can pay for the item (all at once or in installments) in advance of receiving it. After the manufacturer begins the item's production, the contract cannot be canceled. Both parties know exactly what the item will be. No uncertainty can exist.

Joaalah is sometimes called a partnership manufacturing. Joaalah is mostly used to finance the construction of an asset or to finance a manufacturing project. The Joaalah contract is effective when a manufacturer agrees to produce an asset for the buyer at a future date. Both parties agree in advance on the product specifications.

Joaalah is a financial instrument where a manufacturer agrees to complete a construction project on a future date for a fixed, agreed-upon price and with product specifications that both parties agree to. If the project does not fit the contract specifications, the buyer has the right to withdraw from it.

This financial instrument provides for the payment flexibility between the manufacturer and the buyer. The contract does not demand that the buyer pay in advance or that the manufacturer only receive a lump sum at the time of delivery. Instead, both parties can set a schedule of the payment.

Usually, a contract for a not-yet-manufactured product presents some uncertainty about the product. Islamic law prohibits financial institutions from being part of the transactions that involve uncertainty (Gharar). To avoid an uncertainty, the Joaalah contract is as detailed as possible regarding what the end product will be.

In the Joaalah contract, a customer approaches a bank with desired asset's specifications. Both the customer and the bank sign the Joaalah contract, and then the bank manufactures the product or the asset for the customer through its agent such as a manufacturer.

When the bank provides the customer with the Joaalah financial instrument, the customer signs the contract with the bank for the specified asset or project. Then, the bank (via its manufacturing agent) manufactures the asset or project per the customer's specifications. However, in some circumstances the bank does not want to produce the item for the customer. In this case, the bank opts to use two mutually independent Joaalah contracts, called the parallel Joaalah.

Figure 3-6. The Parallel Joaalah Process

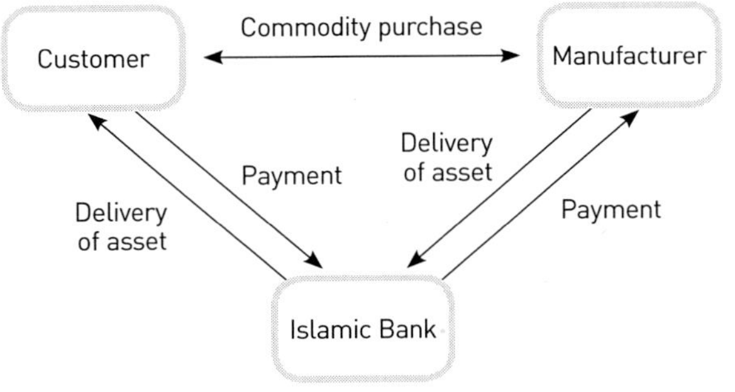

In the case of a parallel Joaalah, the customer who wants the project or asset enters a Joaalah contract with a bank per customer's specifications. The bank then enters into a parallel Joaalah contract with a manufacturer (which is not the bank's agent but a separate third party) to meet those specifications. In theory, when the manufacturer completes the asset or the project, it delivers that product to the bank. In practice, the manufacturer usually delivers the product directly to the customer. The bank pays the manufacturer, and the customer pays the bank according to the agreed payment schedule. The bank marks up the manufacturer's price in the contract with the customer in order to secure a profit.

• **Mosaqat (leasing or renting)**

Mosaqat is a lease or rental contract where one party pays a fixed price for the use of an item over a fixed period of time while the ownership rights and all the liabilities remain with the owner. These contracts are often used to allow someone to lease a car, home, or office building. Specific Mosaqat contracts may ensure that the lessee assumes ownership of the item in question at the end of the lease period.

The Mosaqat contract allows one party to sue an asset owned by another party in exchange for some consideration, usually money. Generally, Mosaqat comes into play when leasing tangible assets.

The Mosaqat means "providing services and goods temporarily for a wage." The Mosaqat contract involves providing products or services on a lease or rental basis. In the Mosaqat contract, a person or party is given the right to use the object for a period of time. The owner retains the ownership of the assets.

The Mosaqat contract is similar to a conventional lease contract in which the owner rents or leases his property or goods to a lessee for a specified number of periods for a fee. For example, the lessee is responsible for major maintenance, just as with many conventional lease contracts. However, the following features of the Mosaqat contract differentiate it from a conventional lease contract:

① The lessor must own the assets for the full lease period.

② If the lessee defaults on payments or delays payments, the lessor cannot charge compound interest.

③ The leased asset's use is specified in the contract.

Three types of Mosaqat arrangements can exist, according to Sharia principles.

① Lease-ending ownership/lease with ownership: In this Mosaqat contract, the lessee owns the leased asset at the end of the lease period. This lease contract does not contain any promise to buy or sell the assets, but the bank may offer a (verbal) unilateral promise of transfer of the ownership or offer a purchase schedule for the asset. The lessee also is allowed to make a (verbal) unilateral promise to purchase the asset. The purchase price is ultimately decided by the market value of the asset or a negotiated price.

② Operating lease: This type of Mosaqat contract does not include the promise to purchase the asset at the end of the contract. Basically, this setup is a hire arrangement with the lessor.

③ Forward lease: This contract is a combination of construction finance and a redeemable leasing agreement. Because this lease is executed for a future date, it is called forward leasing. The forward leasing contract buys out the project (generally a construction project) as a whole at its completion or in tranches (portions) of the project.

Conclusion —

The Islamic banking industry has shown tremendous potential for growth. Iran has completely transformed its banking activities to comply with the accepted Islamic principles. The banking system of Iran is being perceived as an effective tool in pursuit of Islamic economic objectives. But the sector was plagued by slow growth, a large portfolio of non-performing assets, and a narrow range of products and services. There is a need to introduce new products and instruments for the banking system in line with innovations in modern banking. With effective corporate governance and a better interaction with relevant international, regional, and national institutions, Islamic banking in Iran will definitely continue contributing to the welfare of their community, as well as to the welfare of the world as whole.

References

Ahmad, Osman Babikir. (2006). Islamic banking in practice. International Course on: *Principles and practices of Islamic economics and banking*. Baku, Azerbaijan.

Anwar, M. (1992). Islamic banking in Iran and Pakistan: a comparative study. *The Pakistan Development Review*, 31(4), 1089-1097.

Dar, H. (2010). Islamic banking in Iran and Sudan. *Business Asia*, June 27, 2010.

Shahdani, M. S. (2007). Islamic banking in Iran from theory to practice. In *Proceedings of the 2nd Islamic conference.*

Khan, M. S., & Mirakhor, A. (1989). The financial system and monetary policy in an Islamic economy. *Journal of King Abdulaziz University: Islamic Economics*, 1(1), 39-57.

Memon, N. A. (2007). Islamic banking: present and future challenges. *Journal of Management and Social Sciences*, 3(1), 1-10.